TEACHINGS OF THE BUDDHA

Edited by

JACK KORNFIELD

with GIL FRONSDAL

SHAMBHALA

Boston & London

1993

Shambhala Publications, Inc.
Horticultural Hall
300 Massachusetts Avenue
Boston, Massachusetts 02115
www.shambhala.com

© 1993 by Jack Kornfield

Pages 216–218 constitute
an extension of this copyright page.

14   13   12   11   10   9

Printed in Canada
♾ This edition is printed on acid-free paper
that meets the American National Standards
Institute Z39.48 Standard.
Distributed in the United States by Random House, Inc.,
and in Canada by Randon House of Canada Ltd

Cover art: Buddha head, Gandhāra, Kabul Valley,
circa A.D. 4th century

See page 220 for Library of Congress
Cataloging-in-Publication data.

Dedicated to

MAHAGHOSANANDA

A. T. ARIYARATNE

and

TENZIN GYATSO

Who keep the lamp of
the Dharma alive

CONTENTS

EDITOR'S PREFACE

It is said that soon after his enlightenment the Buddha passed a man on the road who was struck by the Buddha's extraordinary radiance and peaceful presence. The man stopped and asked, "My friend, what are you? Are you a celestial being or a god?"

"No," said the Buddha.

"Well, then, are you some kind of magician or wizard?" Again the Buddha answered, "No."

"Are you a man?"

"No."

"Well, my friend, then what are you?" The Buddha replied, "I am awake."

The word *buddha* means "one who is awake." It is the experience of awakening to the truth of life that is offered in the

Buddhist tradition. For twenty-five hundred years the practices and teachings of Buddhism have offered a systematic way to see clearly and live wisely. They have offered a way to discover liberation within our own bodies and minds, in the midst of this very world.

History records that the Buddha was born as a prince in an ancient kingdom of northern India. Although as a youth he was protected by his father in beautiful palaces, as he grew older the Buddha encountered what we must all face: the inevitable sorrows of life. He saw the loss of all things we hold dear, and the aging, sickness, and death that come to every human being. Seeing this, he chose to renounce his royal title and leave his palace to become a seeker of truth, searching for the end of human sorrow, searching for freedom in the face of the ceaseless round of birth and death.

For some years the Buddha practiced as an austere yogi in the forests of India. In time he realized that his extreme asceticism had brought him no more freedom than his previous indulgence in worldly pleasure. Instead, he saw that human freedom must come from practicing a life of inner and outer balance, and he called this discovery the Middle Path.

Having seen this, the Buddha seated himself under a great banyan tree and vowed to find liberation in the face of the forces that bring suffering to humankind. He felt himself assailed by these forces — by fear, attachment, greed, hatred, delusion, temptation, and doubt. The Buddha sat in the midst of these forces with his heart open and his mind clear until he could see to the depths of human consciousness, until he discovered a place of peace at the center of them all. This was his enlightenment, the discovery of *nirvana*,

the freeing of his heart from entanglement
in all the conditions of the world. The realization of truth that he touched that
night was so profound that his teachings
about it have continued to inspire and en-
lighten people all over the world to this
day. Over the centuries, one and a half bil-
lion people, one quarter of the human
race, have followed the Buddha's way.

From the Buddha's enlightenment, two
great powers were awakened in him: transcendent wisdom and universal compassion. Setting in motion the Wheel of the
Dharma, the Buddha wandered first to the
Deer Park in Benares and gave instructions
to the yogis who had practiced with him
in the forest. After this, for forty-five years
he brought the teachings of wisdom and
compassion to all who would listen. These
teachings, which the Buddha called the
Dharma, or Way, are an invitation to follow the path of enlightenment. They are

an invitation to all who hear them to discover their own buddha-nature, the freedom and great heart of compassion that is possible for every human being.

To bring about the awakening of students of all temperaments, the Buddha taught a wonderful variety of spiritual practices. There are foundation practices for the development of loving-kindness, generosity, and moral integrity, the universal ground of spiritual life. Then there is a vast array of meditation practices to train the mind and open the heart. These practices include awareness of the breath and body, mindfulness of feelings and thoughts, practices of *mantra* and devotion, visualization and contemplative reflection, and practices leading to refined and profoundly expanded states of consciousness.

To carry on these teachings, the Buddha created an ordained *sangha,* what is now one of the oldest surviving monastic orders on earth. These monks and nuns, who still number in the hundreds of thousands around the globe, follow the Buddha through a life of renunciation. But the teachings he left were not limited to renunciates. They can be understood and awakened in the heart of human beings in every circumstance, in every walk of life. The essence of these teachings is offered to you in this simple volume.

The first of the texts you will find here were originally recited and passed down orally for six hundred years before being written down. Then they were inscribed on palm leaves in ancient languages such as Pali and Sanskrit, or preserved in translations into Chinese and Tibetan. The passages in the latter portion of this book come from great Indian, Chinese, Japanese, and Tibetan *bodhisattvas,* awakened beings who follow and teach in the spirit of the Buddha. Although these later selections are not from the historical Buddha, they are included for their beauty and the authenticity with which they express the Buddha Dharma. According to Buddhist teachings, the true Buddha is not limited to the body or mind of a particular man who lived long ago. This is illustrated by the tale of a young monk who had spent weeks sitting, enraptured, at the feet of the Buddha, gazing at his form and listening to his words. Finally the Buddha chastised him, saying, "You do not even see me. To see the Buddha, you must see the Dharma, the truth. One who sees the Dharma sees me."

As you read the teachings in this book, remember that they are not meant to be philosophy, poetry, or spiritual studies for you to consider. They are words of truth that can bring you to awakening. Most of these words are so powerful that when they were first spoken, all who were present to hear them were awakened; their eyes and ears opened, and a true inner freedom was discovered.

Go through these pages little by little, savor them in your heart. Let them enter your being and resonate within you, so that you too may be awakened.

May the truth of these verses awaken transcendent wisdom and a great heart of compassion in all beings. May they bring blessings to all.

JACK KORNFIELD
Spirit Rock Center
Woodacre, California
1993

Wakefulness is the way to life.
The fool sleeps
As if he were already dead,
But the master is awake
And he lives forever.

He watches.
He is clear.

How happy he is!
For he sees that wakefulness is life.
How happy he is,
Following the path of the awakened.

With great perseverance
He meditates, seeking
Freedom and happiness.

(from the *Dhammapada,*
translated by Thomas Byrom)

Luminous is this mind, brightly shining, but it is colored by the attachments that visit it. This unlearned people do not really understand, and so do not cultivate the mind. Luminous is this mind, brightly shining, and it is free of the attachments that visit it. This the noble follower of the way really understands; so for them there is cultivation of the mind.

(from the *Anguttara Nikaya*,
translated by Gil Fronsdal)

A person of wisdom should be truthful, without arrogance, without deceit, not slanderous and not hateful. The wise person should go beyond the evil of greed and miserliness.

To have your mind set on calmness, you must take power over sleepiness, drowsiness and lethargy. There is no place for laziness and no recourse to pride.

Do not be led into lying, do not be attached to forms. You must see through all pride and fare along without violence.

Do not get excited by what is old, do not be contented with what is new. Do not grieve for what is lost or be controlled by desire.

(adapted from the *Sutta-nipata*, translated by H. Saddhatissa)

We are what we think.
All that we are arises with our
    thoughts.
With our thoughts we make the
    world.
Speak or act with an impure mind
And trouble will follow you
As the wheel follows the ox that draws
    the cart.

We are what we think.
All that we are arises with our
    thoughts.
With our thoughts we make the
    world.
Speak or act with a pure mind
And happiness will follow you
As your shadow, unshakable.

How can a troubled mind
Understand the way?

Your worst enemy cannot harm you
As much as your own thoughts,
   unguarded.

But once mastered,
No one can help you as much,
Not even your father or your mother.

(from the *Dhammapada*,
translated by Thomas Byrom)

METTA SUTTA

This is the work of those who are skilled and peaceful, who seek the good:

> May they be able and upright, straightforward, of gentle speech and not proud.
> May they be content and easily supported, unburdened, with their senses calmed.
> May they be wise, not arrogant and without desire for the possessions of others.
> May they do nothing mean or that the wise would reprove.

> May all beings be happy.
> May they live in safety and joy.

All living beings, whether weak or strong, tall, stout, average or short, seen or unseen, near or distant, born or to be born, may they all be happy.

Let no one deceive another or despise any being in any state, let none by anger or hatred wish harm to another.

As a mother watches over her child, willing to risk her own life to protect her only child, so with a boundless heart should one cherish all living beings, suffusing the whole world with unobstructed loving kindness.

Standing or walking, sitting or lying down, during all one's waking hours, may one remain mindful of

this heart and this way of living that
is the best in the world.

Unattached to speculations, views and
sense desires, with clear vision, such
a person will never be reborn in the
cycles of suffering.

(version by Gil Fronsdal)

DEVELOPING
LOVING-KINDNESS

Put away all hindrances, let your mind full of love pervade one quarter of the world, and so too the second quarter, and so the third, and so the fourth. And thus the whole wide world, above, below, around and everywhere, altogether continue to pervade with love-filled thought, abounding, sublime, beyond measure, free from hatred and ill-will.

(adapted from the *Digha Nikaya*, translated by Maurice Walshe)

All beings tremble before violence.
All fear death.
All love life.

See yourself in others.
Then whom can you hurt?
What harm can you do?

He who seeks happiness
By hurting those who seek happiness
Will never find happiness.

For your brother is like you.
He wants to be happy.
Never harm him
And when you leave this life
You too will find happiness.

(from the *Dhammapada*,
translated by Thomas Byrom)

The perfume of sandalwood,
Rosebay or jasmine
Cannot travel against the wind.

But the fragrance of virtue
Travels even against the wind,
As far as the ends of the world.

Like garlands woven from a heap of
  flowers,
Fashion from your life as many good
  deeds.

(from the *Dhammapada*,
translated by Thomas Byrom)

GREAT DISCOURSE
ON BLESSINGS

At one time the Exalted One was living in
Jeta Grove. A certain deity of astounding
beauty approached the Exalted One and
said:

Many deities and humans
have pondered on blessings.
Tell me the blessings supreme.

The Buddha replied:

To associate not with the foolish,
to be with the wise,
to honor the worthy ones
this is a blessing supreme.

To reside in a suitable location,
to have good past deeds done,
to set oneself in the right direction
this is a blessing supreme.

To be well spoken, highly trained,
well educated, skilled in handicraft,
and highly disciplined,
this is a blessing supreme.

To be well caring of mother, of father,
to look after wife and children,
to engage in a harmless occupation,
this is a blessing supreme.

Outstanding behavior, blameless action,
open hands to all relatives
and selfless giving,
this is a blessing supreme.

To cease and abstain from evil,
to avoid intoxicants,

to be diligent in virtuous practices,
this is a blessing supreme.

To be reverent and humble,
content and grateful,
to hear the Dharma at the right time,
this is a blessing supreme.

To be patient and obedient,
to visit with spiritual people,
to discuss the Dharma at the right
    time,
this is a blessing supreme.

To live austerely and purely,
to see the noble truths,
and to realize nirvana,
this is the blessing supreme.

A mind unshaken when touched
by the worldly states,

sorrowless, stainless, and secure,
this is the blessing supreme.

Those who have fulfilled all these
are everywhere invincible;
they find well-being everywhere,
theirs is the blessing supreme.

(adapted from *Mangala Sutta*
by Gunaratana Mahathera)

Then the venerable Ananda approached the Lord, prostrated himself and sat down to one side. Sitting there the venerable Ananda said to the Lord:

"Half of this holy life, Lord, is good and noble friends, companionship with the good, association with the good."

"Do not say that, Ananda. Do not say that Ananda. It is the whole of this holy life, this friendship, companionship and association with the good."

(from the *Samyutta Nikaya,*
translated by John Ireland)

How joyful to look upon the
    awakened
And to keep company with the wise.

Follow then the shining ones,
The wise, the awakened, the loving,
For they know how to work and
    forbear.

But if you cannot find
Friend or master to go with you,
Travel on alone—
Like a king who has given away his
    kingdom,
Like an elephant in the forest.

If the traveler can find
A virtuous and wise companion
Let him go with him joyfully
And overcome the dangers of the way.

Follow them
As the moon follows the path of the
    stars.

(from the *Dhammapada*,
translated by Thomas Byrom)

"Look how he abused me and beat
    me,
How he threw me down and robbed
    me."
Live with such thoughts and you
    live in hate.

"Look how he abused me and beat
    me,
How he threw me down and robbed
    me."
Abandon such thoughts, and live in
    love.

In this world
Hate never yet dispelled hate.
Only love dispels hate.
This is the law,
Ancient and inexhaustible.

You too shall pass away.
Knowing this, how can you quarrel?

(from the *Dhammapada*,
translated by Thomas Byrom)

Some children were playing beside a river. They made castles of sand, and each child defended his castle and said, "This one is mine." They kept their castles separate and would not allow any mistakes about which was whose. When the castles were all finished, one child kicked over someone else's castle and completely destroyed it. The owner of the castle flew into a rage, pulled the other child's hair, struck him with his fist and bawled out, "He has spoiled my castle! Come along all of you and help me to punish him as he deserves." The others all came to his help. They beat the child with a stick and then stamped on him as he lay on the ground. . . . Then they went on playing in their sand castles, each saying, "This is mine; no one else may have it. Keep away! Don't touch my castle!" But evening came;

21

it was getting dark and they all thought they ought to be going home. No one now cared what became of his castle. One child stamped on his, another pushed his over with both hands. Then they turned away and went back, each to his home.

(from the *Yogacara Bhumi Sutra*,
translated by Arthur Waley)

The instructed disciple of the Noble Ones does not regard material shape as self, or self as having material shape, or material shape as being in the self, or the self as being in material shape. Nor does he regard feeling, perception, the impulses, or consciousness in any of these ways. He comprehends each of these aggregates as it really is, that it is impermanent, suffering, not-self, compounded, woeful. He does not approach them, grasp after them or determine "Self for me" ["my self"]—and this for a long time conduces to his welfare and happiness.

The instructed disciple of the Noble Ones beholds of material shape and so on: "This is not mine, this am I not, this is not my self." So that when the material shape and so on change and become otherwise there arise not from him grief, sorrow, suffering, lamentation and despair.

(adapted from the *Samyutta Nikaya*, translated by L. Feer)

"To this sage who sees what is good I have come supplicatingly with a question, 'How is anyone to look upon the world so as not to be seen by the king of death?' "

"Look upon the world as void, O Mogharagan," said the Buddha, "being always wakeful; having destroyed the view of oneself as really existing, one may overcome death; the king of death will not see the person who thus regards the world."

(adapted from the *Sutta-nipata,*
translated by V. Fausböll)

"Develop a state of mind like the earth, Rahula. For on the earth people throw clean and unclean things, dung and urine, spittle, pus and blood, and the earth is not troubled or repelled or disgusted. And as you grow like the earth no contacts with pleasant or unpleasant will lay hold of your mind or stick to it.

"Similarly you should develop a state of mind like water, for people throw all manner of clean and unclean things into water and it is not troubled or repelled or disgusted. And similarly with fire, which burns all things, clean and unclean, and with air, which blows upon them all, and with space, which is nowhere established.

"Develop the state of mind of friendliness, Rahula, for, as you do so, ill-will will grow less; and of compassion, for thus vexation will grow less; and of joy, for thus aversion will grow less; and of equanimity, for thus repugnance will grow less.

(from the *Majjhima Nikaya*, translated by A. L. Basham)

Live in joy,
In love,
Even among those who hate.

Live in joy,
In health,
Even among the afflicted.

Live in joy,
In peace,
Even among the troubled.

Look within.
Be still.
Free from fear and attachment,
Know the sweet joy of the way.

(from the *Dhammapada*,
translated by Thomas Byrom)

"I have boiled my rice, I have milked my cows," so said the herdsman Dhaniya. "I am living together with my fellows near the banks of the Mahi river, my house is covered, the fire is kindled: therefore, if thou like, rain, O sky!"

"I am free from anger, free from stubbornness," so said the Blessed One. "I am abiding for one night near the banks of the Mahi river, my house is uncovered, the fire of craving is extinguished: therefore, if thou like, rain, O sky!"

"Gadflies are not to be found with me," so said the herdsman Dhaniya. "In meadows abounding with grass the cows are roaming, and they can endure rain when it comes: therefore, if thou like, rain, O sky!"

"By me is made a well-constructed raft," so said the Buddha. "I have passed over to Nirvana, I have reached the further bank, having overcome the torrent; there is no further use for a raft: therefore, if thou like, rain, O sky!"

"My wife is obedient, not wanton," so said the herdsman Dhaniya. "For a long time she has been living together with me, she is winning, and I hear nothing wicked of her: therefore, if thou like, rain, O sky!"

"My mind is obedient, delivered from all worldliness," so said the Buddha. "It has for a long time been highly cultivated and well-subdued, there is no longer anything wicked in me: therefore, if thou like, rain, O sky!"

"I support myself by my own earning," so said the herdsman Dhaniya. "And my children are all about me, healthy; I hear nothing wicked of them: therefore, if thou like, rain, O sky!"

"I am no one's servant," so said the Buddha. "With what I have gained I wander about in all the world, without being subservient to anyone: therefore, if thou like, rain, O sky!"

(adapted from the *Sutta-nipata,* translated by V. Fausböll)

"Before my enlightenment, while I was still only an unenlightened Bodhisattva, I thought: In the case of material form, of feeling [of pleasure, pain or neither], of perception, of formations, of consciousness, what is the gratification, what is the danger, what is the escape? Then I thought: In the case of each the bodily pleasure and mental joy that arise in dependence on these five aggregates are the gratification; the fact that these things are all impermanent, painful, and subject to change is the danger; the disciplining and abandoning of desire and lust for them is the escape.

"As long as I did not know by direct knowledge, as it actually is, that such was the gratification, such the danger, and such the escape, in the case of these five aggregates affected by clinging, so long did I make no claim to have discovered the enlightenment that is supreme in the world with its deities, its Maras and its divinities, in this generation with its monks and brahmans, with its princes and men. But as soon as I knew by direct knowledge, as it actually is, that such is the gratification, such the danger, and such the escape, in the case of these five aggregates affected by clinging, then I claimed to have discovered the enlightenment that is supreme in the world with its deities, its Maras and its divinities, in this generation with its monks and brahmans, with its princes and men."

"Being myself subject to birth, aging, ailment, death, sorrow, and defilement, seeing danger in what is subject to those things and seeking the unborn, unaging, unailing, deathless, sorrowless, undefiled supreme surcease of bondage, nirvana, I attained it. The knowledge and vision was in me: My deliverance is unassailable; this is my last birth; there is now no renewal of being."

"Seeking but not finding the House Builder,
I traveled through the round of countless births:
O painful is birth ever and again.
House Builder, you have now been seen;
You shall not build the house again.
Your rafters have been broken down;
Your ridge pole is demolished too.
My mind has now attained the unformed nirvana
And reached the end of every kind of craving."

(from the *Samyutta Nikaya*,
Majjhima Nikaya, and *Dhammapada*,
translated by Nyanamoli Thera)

A man approached the Blessed One and wanted to have all his philosophical questions answered before he would practice.

In response, the Buddha said, "It is as if a man had been wounded by a poisoned arrow and when attended to by a physician were to say, 'I will not allow you to remove this arrow until I have learned the caste, the age, the occupation, the birthplace, and the motivation of the person who wounded me.' That man would die before having learned all this. In exactly the same way, anyone who should say, 'I will not follow the teaching of the Blessed One until the Blessed One has explained all the multiform truths of the world'—that person would die before the Buddha had explained all this."

(adapted from the *Majjhima Nikaya*, translated by H. C. Warren)

"Just as a capable physician might instantly cure a patient who is in pain and seriously ill; so also, dear sir, whatever one hears of the Buddha's Dharma, be it discourses, mixed prose, explanations or marvelous statements, one's sorrow, lamentation, pain, grief and despair will vanish.

"Just as if there were a beautiful pond with a pleasant shore, its water being clear, agreeable, cool and transparent, and a man came by, scorched and exhausted by the heat, fatigued, parched and thirsty, and he would step into the pond, bathe and drink, and thus all his plight, fatigue and feverishness are allayed; so also, dear sir, whenever one hears the Buddha's Dharma, be it discourses, mixed prose, explanations or marvelous statements, all one's plight, fa-

tigue and the feverish burning of the heart
are allayed."

(from the *Anguttara Nikaya*,
translated by Nyanaponika Thera)

THE FOUR NOBLE TRUTHS

The Buddha said,

"And I discovered that profound truth, so difficult to perceive, difficult to understand, tranquillizing and sublime, which is not to be gained by mere reasoning, and is visible only to the wise.

"The world, however, is given to pleasure, delighted with pleasure, enchanted with pleasure. Truly, such beings will hardly understand the law of conditionality, the dependent origination of everything. Yet there are beings whose eyes are only a little covered with dust: they will understand the truth."

What now is the Noble Truth of Suffering?

Birth is suffering; decay is suffering; death

is suffering; sorrow, lamentation, pain, grief, and despair are suffering; not to get what one desires is suffering; in short the five groups of existence are suffering.

What, now, is the Noble Truth of the Origin of Suffering?

It is craving, which gives rise to fresh rebirth, and, bound up with pleasure and lust, now here, now there, finds ever-fresh delight. But where does this craving arise and take root? Wherever in the world there are delightful and pleasurable things, there this craving rises and takes root. Eye, ear, nose, tongue, body, and mind are delightful and pleasurable: there this craving arises and takes root.

Visual objects, sounds, smells, tastes, bodily impressions, and mind objects are delightful and pleasurable: there this craving arises and takes root.

Consciousness, sense impression, feeling born of sense impression, perception,

will, craving, thinking, and reflection are
delightful and pleasurable: there this craving arises and takes root.

What, now, is the Noble Truth of the
Extinction of Suffering?

It is the complete fading away and extinction of this craving, its forsaking and
abandonment, liberation and detachment
from it. The extinction of greed, the extinction of hate, the extinction of delusion:
this, indeed, is called Nirvana.

And for a disciple thus freed, in whose
heart dwells peace, there is nothing to be
added to what has been done, and naught
more remains to do. Just as a rock of one
solid mass remains unshaken by the wind,
even so neither forms, nor sounds, nor
odors, nor tastes, nor contacts of any kind,
neither the desired nor the undesired can
cause such a one to waver; one is steadfast
in mind, gained is deliverance.

And one who has considered all the contrasts of this earth, and is no more disturbed by anything whatever in the world, the Peaceful One, freed from rage, from sorrow, and from longing, has passed beyond birth and decay.

This I call neither arising, nor passing away, neither standing still, nor being born, nor dying. There is neither foothold, nor development, nor any basis. This is the end of suffering.

Hence, the purpose of the Holy Life does not consist in acquiring alms, honor, or fame, nor in gaining morality, concentration, or the eye of knowledge. That unshakable deliverance of the heart: that, indeed, is the object of the Holy Life, that is its essence, that is its goal.

What, now, is the Noble Truth of the Path that leads to the extinction of suffering?

To give oneself up to indulgence in sensual pleasure, the base, common, vulgar, unholy, unprofitable; or to give oneself up to self-mortification, the painful, unholy, unprofitable: both these two extremes, the Perfect One has avoided, and has found out the Middle Path, which makes one both see and know, which leads to peace, to discernment, to Nirvana.

It is the Noble Eightfold Path, the way that leads to the extinction of suffering, namely:

1. Right Understanding
2. Right Thought
3. Right Speech
4. Right Action
5. Right Livelihood
6. Right Effort
7. Right Mindfulness
8. Right Concentration

This is the Middle Path which the Perfect One has found out, which makes one both see and know, which leads to peace, to discernment, to enlightenment.

(from the *Samyutta Nikaya*, translated by Nyanatiloka)

Did you ever see in the world a man, or a woman, eighty, ninety, or a hundred years old, frail, crooked as a gable-roof, bent down, resting on crutches, with tottering steps, infirm, youth long since fled, with broken teeth, gray and scanty hair or none, wrinkled, with blotched limbs? And did the thought never come to you that you also are subject to decay, that you also cannot escape it?

Did you ever see in the world a man, or a woman who, being sick, afflicted, and grievously ill, wallowing in his own filth, was lifted up by some and put to bed by others? And did the thought never come to you that you also are subject to disease, that you also cannot escape it?

Did you never see in the world the corpse of a man, or a woman, one or two or three days after death, swollen up, blue-black in color, and full of corruption? And did the thought never come to you that you also are subject to death, that you also cannot escape it?

Suppose a man who was not blind beheld the many bubbles on the Ganges as they drove along, and he watched them and carefully examined them, then after he had carefully examined them they would appear to him empty, unreal and unsubstantial. In exactly the same way does the monk behold all physical phenomena, feelings, perceptions, mental formations, and states of consciousness—whether they be of the past, or the present, or the future, far or near. And he watches them, and examines them carefully; and, after carefully examining them, they appear to him empty, void and without a Self.

(from the *Majjhima Nikaya,*
translated by Nyanatiloka)

Few cross over the river.
Most are stranded on this side.
On the riverbank they run up and
    down.

But the wise person, following the
    way,
Crosses over, beyond the reach of
    death.

Free from desire,
Free from possessions,
Free from attachment and appetite,
Following the seven lights of
    awakening,
And rejoicing greatly in his freedom,
In this world the wise person

Becomes themself a light,
Pure, shining, free.

(adapted from the *Dhammapada*,
translated by Thomas Byrom)

Gotami was her family name, but because she tired easily, she was called Kisa Gotami, or Frail Gotami. She was reborn at Savatthi in a poverty-stricken house. When she grew up, she married, going to the house of her husband's family to live. There, because she was the daughter of a poverty-stricken house, they treated her with contempt. After a time she gave birth to a son. Then they accorded her respect.

But when that boy of hers was old enough to play and run hither and about, he died. Sorrow sprang up within her. Thought she: Since the birth of my son, I, who was once denied honor and respect in this very house, have received respect. These folk may even seek to cast my son away. Taking her son on her hip, she went about from one house door to another, saying: "Give me medicine for my son!"

Wherever people encountered her, they said, Where did you ever meet with medicine for the dead? So saying, they clapped their hands and laughed in derision. She had not the slightest idea what they meant.

Now a certain wise man saw her and thought: This woman must have been driven out of her mind by sorrow for her son. But medicine for her, no one else is likely to know—the Sage of the Ten Forces alone is likely to know. Said he: "Woman, as for medicine for your son— there is no one else who knows—the Sage of the Ten Forces, the foremost individual in the world of men and the worlds of the gods, resides at a neighboring monastery. Go to him and ask."

The man speaks the truth, thought she. Taking her son on her hip, she took her stand in the outer circle of the congregation around the seated Buddha and said:

"O Exalted One, give me medicine for my son!"

The Teacher, seeing that she was ripe for conversion, said: "You did well, Gotami, in coming hither for medicine. Go enter the city, make the rounds of the entire city, beginning at the beginning, and in whatever house no one has ever died, from that house fetch tiny grains of mustard seed."

"Very well, reverend sir," said she. Delighted in heart, she entered within the city, and at the very first house said: "The Sage of the Ten Forces bids me fetch tiny grains of mustard seed for medicine for my son. Give me tiny grains of mustard seed."

"Alas! Gotami," said they, and brought and gave to her.

"This particular seed I cannot take. In this house someone has died!"

"What say you, Gotami! Here it is impossible to count the dead!"

"Well then, enough! I'll not take it. The Sage of the Ten Forces did not tell me to take mustard seed from a house where anyone has ever died."

In this same way she went to the second house, and to the third. Thought she: In the entire city this must be the way! The Buddha, full of compassion for the welfare of mankind, must have seen! Overcome with emotion, she went outside of the city, carried her son to the burning-ground, and holding him in her arms, said: "Dear little son, I thought that you alone had been overtaken by this thing which men call death. But you are not the only one death has overtaken. This is a law common to all mankind." So saying, she cast her son away in the burning-ground. Then she uttered the following stanza:

No village law, no law of market town,
No law of a single house is this—

Of all the world and all the worlds of
   gods
This only is the Law, that all things are
   impermanent.

(from *Buddhist Parables*,
translated by E. W. Burlingame)

TEACHINGS OF THE BUDDHA

"All formations are transient; all formations are subject to suffering; all things are without a self.

"Therefore, whatever there be of form, of feeling, perception, mental formations, or consciousness, whether past, present, or future, one's own or external, gross or subtle, lofty or low, far or near, one should understand according to reality and true wisdom: 'This does not belong to me; this am I not; this is not my Self.'"

(from the *Anguttara Nikaya* and *Samyutta Nikaya*, translated by Nyanatiloka)

"Just so, Ananda, in one who contemplates the enjoyment of all things that make for clinging, craving arises; through craving, clinging is conditioned; through clinging, the process of becoming is conditioned; through the process of becoming, rebirth is conditioned; through rebirth are conditioned old age and death, sorrow, lamentation, pain, grief, and despair. Thus arises the whole mass of suffering again in the future.

"But in the person, Ananda, who dwells contemplating the misery of all things that make for clinging, craving ceases; when craving ceases, clinging ceases; when clinging ceases, the process of becoming ceases; when the process of becoming ceases, rebirth ceases; when rebirth ceases, old age and death, sorrow, lamentation, pain, grief and despair cease. Thus the entire mass of suffering ceases.

"Suppose, Ananda, there were a great tree and a man were to come with an axe and basket and were to cut down that tree at the root. After cutting it at the root he were to dig a trench and were to pull out the roots even to the rootlets and fibers of them. Then he were to cut the tree into logs and were then to split the logs and were then to make the logs into chips. Then he were to dry the chips in wind and sun, then burn them with fire, collect them into a heap of ash, then winnow the ashes in a strong wind or let them be carried away by the swift stream of a river.

"Surely that great tree thus cut down at the roots would be made as a palmtree stump, become unproductive, become unable to sprout again in the future.

"Just so, Ananda, in him who dwells contemplating the misery of all things that make for clinging . . . the entire mass of suffering ceases."

(from the *Samyutta Nikaya*,
translated by David Maurice)

THE SUTRA ON TOTALITY

Monks, I will teach you the totality of life. Listen, attend carefully to it and I will speak.

What, monks, is totality? It is just the eye with the objects of sight, the ear with the objects of hearing, the nose with the objects of smell, the body with the objects of touch and the mind with the objects of cognition. This, monks, is called totality.

Now, if anyone were to say, "Aside from this explanation of totality, I will preach another totality," that person would be speaking empty words, and being questioned would not be able to answer. Why is this? Because that person is talking about something outside of possible knowledge.

(from the *Samyutta Nikaya*, translated by Gil Fronsdal)

THE FIRE SERMON

And the Blessed One went forth to Gaya-sisa, near Gaya, together with one thousand monks.

There the Blessed One thus addressed the monks: "Everything, O monks, is burning. And how, O monks is everything burning?

"The eye, O monks, is burning; visible things are burning; the mental impressions based on the eye are burning; the contact of the eye with visible things is burning; the sensation produced by the contact of the eye with visible things, be it pleasant, be it painful, be it neither pleasant nor painful, that also is burning. With what fire is it burning? I declare unto you that it is burning with the fire of greed, with the fire of anger, with the fire of igno-

rance; it is burning with the anxieties of
birth, decay, death, grief, lamentation, suffering, dejection, and despair.

"The ear is burning, sounds are
burning, . . . The nose is burning, odors
are burning, . . . The tongue is burning,
tastes are burning, . . . The body is burning, objects of contact are burning, . . . The
mind is burning, thoughts are burning, all
are burning with the fire of greed, of anger, and of ignorance.

"Considering this, O monks, a disciple
walking in the Noble Path, becomes weary
of the eye, weary of visible things, weary
of the mental impressions based on the
eye, weary of the contact of the eye with
visible things, weary also of the sensation
produced by the contact of the eye with
visible things, be it pleasant, be it painful,
be it neither pleasant nor painful. He becomes weary of the ear, and so forth . . .
down to . . . thoughts. Becoming weary of

all that, he divests himself of grasping; by absence of grasping he is made free; when he is free, he becomes aware that he is free; and he realizes that rebirth is exhausted; and that there is no further return to this world."

When this exposition was propounded, the minds of those thousand monks became free from attachment to the world, and were released from all entanglement.

(adapted from the *Mahavagga*,
translated by T. W. Rhys-Davids
and Herman Oldenberg)

Master your senses,
What you taste and smell,
What you see, what you hear.

In all things be a master
Of what you do and say and think.
Be free.

Are you quiet?
Quieten your body.
Quieten your mind.

By your own efforts
Waken yourself, watch yourself,
And live joyfully.

Follow the truth of the way.
Reflect upon it.
Make it your own.
Live it.
It will always sustain you.

(from the *Dhammapada*,
translated by Thomas Byrom)

Nagasena said:

"Nirvana shares one quality with the lotus, two with water, three with medicine, ten with space, three with the wishing jewel, and five with a mountain peak. As the lotus is unstained by water, so is Nirvana unstained by all the defilements. As cool water allays feverish heat, so also Nirvana is cool and allays the fever of all the passions. Moreover, as water removes the thirst of men and beasts who are exhausted, parched, thirsty, and overpowered by heat, so also Nirvana removes the craving for sensuous enjoyments, the craving for further becoming, the craving for the cessation of becoming. As medicine protects from the torments of poison, so Nirvana from the torments of the poisonous passions. Moreover, as medicine puts an end to sickness, so Nirvana to all sufferings. Finally, Nirvana and medicine both give security. And these are the ten qualities which Nirvana shares with space. Neither is born, grows old, dies, passes away, or is reborn; both are unconquerable, cannot be stolen, are unsupported, are roads respectively for birds and Awakened Ones to journey on, are unobstructed and infinite. Like the wishing jewel, Nirvana grants all one can desire, brings joy, and sheds light. As a mountain peak is lofty and exalted, so is Nirvana. As a mountain peak is unshakable, so is Nirvana. As a mountain peak is inaccessible, so is Nirvana inaccessible to all the passions. As no seeds can grow on a mountain peak, so the seeds of all the passions cannot grow in Nirvana. And finally, as a mountain peak is free from all desire to please or displease, so is Nirvana."

(from the *Milindapanha,* translated by Edward Conze)

Love yourself and be awake—
Today, tomorrow, always.

First establish yourself in the way,
Then teach others,
And so defeat sorrow.

To straighten the crooked
You must first do a harder thing—
Straighten yourself.

You are your only master.
Who else?
Subdue yourself,
And discover your master.

(adapted from the *Dhammapada*,
translated by Thomas Byrom)

At that time, being the sowing season, five hundred ploughs owned by the brahmin Kasibharadvaja were set to work. In the morning then, the Buddha, having robed himself and taking his bowl and double-layered robe, went to that place where Kasibharadvaja's work was in progress. It was lunch time and the food was being distributed by the brahmin. When the Buddha arrived at the place where the food was being distributed he stood aside. The brahmin, seeing the Buddha standing for alms, said thus: "O recluse, I plough and sow, and having ploughed and sown, I eat. You also, recluse, should plough and sow; and having ploughed and sown, you should eat."

"I too, brahmin, plough and sow; and having ploughed and sown, I eat."

"We see neither yoke, nor plough, nor

ploughshare, nor goad, nor oxen of the Venerable Gotama, and yet you say: 'I too, brahmin, plough and sow; and having ploughed and sown, I eat.'" Thereupon Kasibharadvaja addressed the Buddha in this stanza:

"You claim to be a farmer, yet we do not see your ploughing. Being questioned by us about your ploughing, tell us in such a manner that we may know of it."

The Buddha said thus:

"Confidence is the seed; self-control the rein; wisdom my yoke and plough; modesty is my pole; mind is the rope; mindfulness my ploughshare and goad.

"Bodily action is well-guarded, speech is well-guarded, moderate in food, I make truth the destroyer of weeds and calm my release.

"Exertion is my yoked-oxen which carries me toward Nirvana. It goes onward without stopping; having gone there one has no regrets.

"In this way the ploughing is done; it bears the fruit of immortality. Having accomplished this ploughing, one becomes free from all suffering."

(from the *Sutta-nipata*,
translated by H. Saddhatissa)

Drink deeply.
Live in serenity and joy.
The wise person delights in the truth
And follows the law of the awakened.

The farmer channels water to his land
The fletcher whittles his arrows.
And the carpenter turns his wood.
So the wise direct their mind.

(adapted from the *Dhammapada*,
translated by Thomas Byrom)

THE PATH OF MINDFULNESS

"O monks," said the Buddha, "there is a most wonderful way to help living beings realize purification, overcome directly grief and sorrow, end pain and anxiety, travel the right path, and realize nirvana. This way is the Four Establishments of Mindfulness.

"What are the Four Establishments?

"Monks, a practitioner remains established in the observation of the body in the body, diligent, with clear understanding, mindful, having abandoned every craving and every distaste for this life.

"One remains established in the observation of the feelings in the feelings, diligent, with clear understanding, mindful, having abandoned craving and every distaste for this life.

"One remains established in the observation of the mind in the mind, diligent, with clear understanding, mindful, having abandoned every craving and every distaste for this life.

"One remains established in the observation of the objects of mind in the objects of mind, diligent, with clear understanding, mindful, having abandoned every craving and every distaste for this life."

"And how does a practitioner remain established in the observation of the body in the body?

"One goes to the forest, to the foot of a tree, or to an empty room, sits down cross-legged in the lotus position, holds one's body straight, and establishes mindfulness in front of oneself. "Breathing in, one is aware of breathing in. Breathing out, one is aware of breathing out. Breathing in a long breath, one knows, 'I am breathing in a long breath.' Breathing out a long breath, one knows, 'I am breathing out a long breath.' Breathing in a short breath, one knows, 'I am breathing in a short breath.' Breathing out a short breath, one knows, 'I am breathing out a short breath.'

"The practitioner uses the following practice: 'Breathing in, I am aware of my whole body. Breathing out, I am aware of my whole body.' And then, 'Breathing in, I calm the activities of my body. Breathing out, I calm the activities of my body.'

"Moreover, when walking, the practitioner is aware, 'I am walking'; when standing is aware, 'I am standing'; when sitting, is aware, 'I am sitting'; when lying down, is aware, 'I am lying down.' In whatever position one's body happens to be, one is aware of the position of the body.

"When the one is going forward or backward, one applies full awareness to one's going forward or backward. When one looks in front or looks behind, bends down or stands up, one also applies full awareness to what one is doing. One applies full awareness to wearing the robe or carrying the alms bowl. When one eats or drinks, chews or savors the food, one applies full awareness to all this. When passing excrement or urinating, one applies full awareness to this. When one walks, stands, lies down, sits, sleeps or wakes up, speaks or is silent, one shines his awareness on all this."

"Monks, how does a practitioner remain established in the observation of the feelings in the feelings?

"Whenever the practitioner has a pleasant feeling, one is aware, 'I am experiencing a pleasant feeling.' Whenever one has a painful feeling, one is aware, 'I am experiencing a painful feeling.' Whenever one experiences a feeling which is neither pleasant nor painful, one is aware, 'I am experiencing a neutral feeling.' When one experiences a feeling based in the body, one is aware, 'I am experiencing a feeling based in the body.' When one experiences a feeling based in the mind, one is aware, 'I am experiencing a feeling based in the mind.' "

"Monks, how does a practitioner remain established in the observation of the mind in the mind?

"When one's mind is desiring, the practitioner is aware, 'My mind is desiring.' When one's mind is not desiring, one is aware, 'My mind is not desiring.' When one's mind is hating something, one is aware, 'My mind is hating.' When one's mind is not hating, one is aware, 'My mind is not hating.' When one's mind is in a state of ignorance, one is aware,

'My mind is in a state of ignorance.' When one's mind is not in a state of ignorance, one is aware, 'My mind is not in a state of ignorance.' When one's mind is tense, one is aware, 'My mind is tense.' When one's mind is not tense, one is aware, 'My mind is not tense.' When one's mind is distracted, one is aware, 'My mind is distracted.' When one's mind is not distracted, one is aware, 'My mind is not distracted.' When one's mind has a wider scope, one is aware, 'My mind has widened in scope.' When one's mind has a narrow scope, one is aware, 'My mind has become narrow in scope.'

"When one's mind is composed, one is aware, 'My mind is composed.' When one's mind is not composed, one is aware, 'My mind is not composed.' When one's mind is free, one is aware, 'My mind is free.' When one's mind is not free, one is aware, 'My mind is not free.' "

"How, monks, does the practitioner remain established in the observation of the Four Noble Truths?

"A practitioner is aware 'This is suffering,' as it arises. One is aware, 'This is the cause of the suffering,' as it arises. One is aware, 'This is the end of suffering,' as it arises. One is aware, 'This is the path which leads to the end of suffering,' as it arises."

"Monks, one who practices in the Four Establishments of Mindfulness for seven years can expect one of two fruits—the highest understanding in this very life or, if there remains some residue of affliction, he can attain the fruit of no-return.

"Let alone seven years, monks, whoever practices in the Four Establishments of Mindfulness for six, five, four, three, two years, one year, or one month, can also expect one of two fruits—either the highest understanding in this very life or can attain the fruit of no-return.

"Let alone a month, monks, whoever practices the Four Establishments of Mindfulness one week can also expect one of two fruits—either the highest understanding in this very life or the fruit of no-return."

The monks were delighted to hear the teaching of the Buddha. They took it to heart and began to put it into practice.

(adapted from *Satipatthana-sutta,* translated by Thich Nhat Hanh and Annabel Laity)

However young,
The seeker who sets out upon the way
Shines bright over the world.

But day and night
The man who is awake
Shines in the radiance of the spirit.

Meditate.
Live purely.
Be quiet.
Do your work, with mastery.

Like the moon,
Come out from behind the clouds!
Shine.

(from the *Dhammapada*,
translated by Thomas Byrom)

Then, Bahiya, thus must you train your-self: In the seen there will be just the seen, in the heard just the heard, in the sensed just the sensed, in the imagined just the imagined. Thus you will have no "thereby." That is how you must train yourself. Now, Bahiya, when in the seen there will be to you just the seen, in the heard just the heard, in the imagined just the imagined, in the cognized just the cognized, then, Bahiya, as you will have no "thereby," you will have no "therein." As you, Bahiya, will have no "therein," it follows that you will have no "here" or "beyond" or "midway between." That is just the end of Ill.

(adapted from the *Udana*,
translated by F. L. Woodward)

THE SUTRA ON
FULL AWARENESS
OF BREATHING

When the full moon day arrived, the Buddha, seated under the open sky, looked over the assembly and said:

"O followers of the way, the method of being fully aware of breathing, if developed and practiced continuously, will have great rewards and bring great advantages. It will lead to success in the practice of the Seven Factors of Awakening. The Seven Factors of Awakening, if developed and practiced continuously, will give rise to Understanding and Liberation of the Mind.

"What is the way to develop and practice continuously the method of Full Awareness of Breathing so that the practice will be rewarding and offer great benefit?

"It is like this, the practitioner goes into the forest or to the foot of a tree, or to any deserted place, and sits stably in the lotus position, holding one's body quite straight. Breathing in, one knows that one is breathing in; and breathing out, one knows that one is breathing out.

"Breathing in a long breath, one knows, 'I am breathing in a long breath.' Breathing out a long breath, one knows, 'I am breathing out a long breath.'

"Breathing in a short breath, one knows, 'I am breathing in a short breath.' Breathing out a short breath, one knows, 'I am breathing out a short breath.'

"'I am breathing in and am aware of my whole body. I am breathing out and am aware of my whole body.' This is how one practices.

"'I am breathing in and making whole body calm and at peace. breathing out and making my who'

calm and at peace.' This is how one practices.

"'I am breathing in and feeling joyful. I am breathing out and feeling joyful.' This is how one practices.

"'I am breathing in and feeling happy. I am breathing out and feeling happy.' One practices like this.

"'I am breathing in and am aware of the activities of the mind in me. I am breathing out and am aware of the activities of the mind in me.' One practices like this.

"'I am breathing in and making the activities of the mind in me calm and at peace. I am breathing out and making the activities of the mind in me calm and at peace.' One practices like this.

"'I am breathing in and am aware of my mind. I am breathing out and am aware of my mind.' One practices like this.

"'I am breathing in and making my mind happy and at peace. I am breathing

out and making my mind happy and at peace.' One practices like this.

"'I am breathing in and concentrating my mind. I am breathing out and concentrating my mind.' One practices like this.

"'I am breathing in and liberating my mind. I am breathing out and liberating my mind.' One practices like this.

"'I am breathing in and observing the impermanent nature of all dharmas. I am breathing out and observing the impermanent nature of all dharmas.' One practices like this.

"'I am breathing in and observing the fading of all dharmas. I am breathing out and observing the fading of all dharmas.' One practices like this.

"'I am breathing in and contemplating liberation. I am breathing out and contemplating liberation.' One practices like this.

"'I am breathing in and contemplating

letting go. I am breathing out and contemplating letting go.' One practices like this.

"The Full Awareness of Breathing, if developed and practiced continuously according to these instructions, will be rewarding and of great benefit."

(adapted from *The Sutra on Full Awareness of Breathing*, translated by Thich Nhat Hanh)

Friends, I know nothing which is as intractable as an untamed heart. The untamed heart is indeed intractable.

Friends, I know nothing which is as tractable as a tamed heart. The tamed heart is indeed tractable.

Friends, I know nothing which tends toward loss as does an untamed heart. Indeed, the untamed heart tends toward loss.

Friends, I know nothing which tends toward growth as does a tamed heart. Indeed, the tamed heart tends toward growth.

Friends, I know nothing which brings suffering as does an untamed, uncontrolled, unattended and unrestrained heart. Such a heart brings suffering.

Friends, I know nothing which brings joy

as does a tamed, controlled, attended and restrained heart. Such a heart brings joy.

(from the *Anguttara Nikaya*,
translated by Gil Fronsdal)

THE PARABLE OF THE LUTE

Once the Blessed One lived near Rajagaha, on Vulture Peak. At that time while the venerable Sona lived alone and secluded in the Cool Forest, this thought occurred to him:

"Of those disciples of the Blessed One who are energetic, I am one. Yet, my mind has not found freedom."

Now the Blessed One, perceiving in his own mind the venerable Sona's thoughts, left Vulture Peak, and, as speedily as a strong man might stretch his bent arm or bend his stretched arm, he appeared in the Cool Forest before the venerable Sona. And he said to the venerable Sona:

"Sona, did not this thought arise in your mind: 'Of those disciples of the

Blessed One who are energetic, I am one. Yet, my mind has not found freedom.' "

"Yes, Lord."

"Tell me, Sona, in earlier days were you not skilled in playing string music on a lute?"

"Yes, Lord."

"And tell me, Sona, when the strings of your lute were too taut, was then your lute tuneful and easily playable?"

"Certainly not, O Lord."

"And when the strings of your lute were too loose, was then your lute tuneful and easily playable?"

"Certainly not, O Lord."

"But when, Sona, the strings of your lute were neither too taut nor too loose, but adjusted to an even pitch, did your lute then have a wonderful sound and was it easily playable?"

"Certainly, O Lord."

"Similarly, Sona, if energy is applied too

strongly, it will lead to restlessness, and if energy is too lax it will lead to lassitude. Therefore, Sona, keep your energy in balance and balance the Spiritual Faculties and in this way focus your attention."

"Yes, O Lord," replied the venerable Sona in assent.

Afterward the venerable Sona kept his energy balanced, balanced the Spiritual Faculties and in this way focused his attention. And the venerable Sona, living alone and secluded, diligent, ardent and resolute, soon realized here and now, through his own direct knowledge, that unequaled goal of the holy life.

(adapted from the *Anguttara Nikaya*, translated by Nyanaponika Thera)

As in the ocean's midmost depth no wave is born, but all is still, so let the practitioner be still, be motionless, and nowhere should one swell.

(from the *Sutta-nipata,* translated by Dines Anderson and Helmer Smith)

"Endowed with this noble aggregate of moral discipline, this noble restraint over the sense faculties, this noble mindfulness and clear comprehension, and this noble contentment, a monk resorts to a secluded dwelling, sits down, crosses his legs, holds his body erect, and sets up mindfulness before him.

"Having abandoned covetousness for the world, he dwells with a mind free from covetousness; he purifies his mind from covetousness. Having abandoned ill will and hatred, he dwells with a benevolent mind, sympathetic for the welfare of all living beings; he purifies his mind from ill will and hatred. Having abandoned dullness and drowsiness, he dwells perceiving light, mindful and clearly comprehending; he purifies his mind from dullness and drowsiness. Having abandoned restlessness and worry, he dwells at ease within himself, with a peaceful mind; he purifies his mind from restlessness and worry. Having abandoned doubt, he dwells as one who has passed beyond doubt, unperplexed about wholesome states; he purifies his mind from doubt.

"Suppose a man were to become sick, afflicted, gravely ill, so that he could not enjoy his food and his strength would decline. After some time he would recover from that illness and would enjoy his food and regain his bodily strength. He would reflect on this, and as a result he would become glad and experience joy.

"Again, suppose a man were a slave, without independence, subservient to others, unable to go where he wants. After some time he would be released from slavery and gain his independence; he would no longer be subservient to others but a free man able to go where he wants. He would reflect on this, and as a result he would become glad and experience joy.

"Again, suppose a man with wealth and possessions were traveling along a desert road where food was scarce and dangers were many. After some time he would cross over the desert and arrive safely at a village which is safe and free from danger. He would reflect on this, and as a result he would become glad and experience joy.

"When he sees that these five hindrances have been abandoned within himself, he regards that as freedom from debt, as good health, as release from prison, as freedom from slavery, as a place of safety."

(from the *Digha Nikaya*,
translated by Bhikkhu Bodhi)

SONGS OF THE NUNS

Free woman,
be free
as the moon is freed
from the eclipse of the sun.

With a free mind,
in no debt,
enjoy what has been given to you.

Get rid of the tendency
to judge yourself
above, below, or
equal to others.
A nun who has self-possession
and integrity
will find the peace that nourishes
and never causes surfeit.

Be filled with all good things
like the moon on the fifteenth day.
Completely, perfectly full
of wisdom
tear open
the massive dark.

I am a nun, trained and self-composed,
established mindfulness
and entered peace like an arrow.
The elements of body and mind grew
    still,
happiness came.

Everywhere clinging to pleasure is
    destroyed,
the great dark is torn apart,
and Death,
you too are destroyed.

(from the *Therigatha*,
translated by Susan Murcott)

There is no fire like greed,
No crime like hatred,
No sorrow like separation,
No sickness like hunger of
    heart,
An no joy like the joy of
    freedom.

Health, contentment and trust
Are your greatest possessions,
And freedom your greatest joy.

Look within.
Be still.
Free from fear and
    attachment,
Know the sweet joy of living in
    the way.

(adapted from the *Dhammapada*,
    translated by Thomas Byrom)

On a certain occasion, the Exalted One was dwelling in the Sumbha country, in a township of the Sumbhas, called Sedaka. There the Exalted One addressed the monks:

"Once upon a time, monks, a bamboo-acrobat set up his pole and called to his pupil, Medakathalika, saying: 'Come, my lad, Medakathalika, climb the pole and stand on my shoulders!'

"'All right, master,' replied the pupil to the bamboo-acrobat. The student then climbed the pole and stood on his master's shoulder. Then, monks, the bamboo-acrobat said to his pupil: 'Now Medakathalika, my lad, you protect me well and I shall protect you. Thus watched and warded by each other, we will show our tricks, get a good fee, and come down safe from the bamboo-pole.'

"At these words Medakathalika the pupil said to the bamboo-acrobat: 'No, no! That won't do, master! You look after yourself, master, and I'll look after myself. Thus watched and warded each by himself, we'll show our tricks, get a good fee, and come down safe from the bamboo-pole.'

"Therein that is the right way," said the Exalted One, "Just as Medakathalika the pupil said to his master, 'I'll protect myself,' so, monks, should the Foundation of Mindfulness be practiced. 'I'll protect others': so should the Foundations of Mindfulness be practiced. Protecting onself, monks, one protects others; protecting others, one protects oneself.

"And how, monks, does one, in protecting oneself, protect others? By frequent practice, development and making much of the Foundations of Mindfulness. Thus, monks, in protecting oneself one protects others.

"And how, monks, does one, in protecting others, protect oneself? By forbearance, by nonviolence, by loving-kindness, by compassion. Thus, monks, in protecting others, one protects onself.

"'I shall protect myself': with this intention, monks, the Foundations of Mindfulness should be practiced. 'I shall protect others': with this intention the Foundations of Mindfulness should be practiced. Protecting oneself, one protects others; protecting others, one protects oneself."

(adapted from the *Samyutta Nikaya*, translated by John Ireland)

THE PARABLE OF THE RAFT

"Monks, I will teach you the parable of the raft—for getting across, not for retaining. It is like a man who going on a journey sees a great stretch of water, the near bank with dangers and fears, the farther bank secure and without fears, but there is neither a boat for crossing over, nor a bridge across. It occurs to him that to cross over from the perils of this bank to the security of the farther bank, he should fashion a raft out of sticks and branches and depending on the raft, cross over to safety. When he has done this it occurs to him that the raft has been very useful and he wonders if he ought to take it with him on his head or shoulders. What do you think, monks? That the man is doing what should be done to the raft?"

"No, lord."

"What should that man do, monks? When he has crossed over to the beyond he must leave the raft and proceed on his journey. Monks, a man doing this would be doing what should be done to the raft. In this way I have taught you Dharma, like the parable of the raft, for getting across, not for retaining. You, monks, by understanding the parable of the raft, must not cling to right states of mind and, all the more, to wrong states of mind."

(adapted from the *Majjhima Nikaya*, translated by Christmas Humphreys)

THE KALAMAS' DILEMMA

One time Buddha was walking on tour with a large group of monks, when he came to a town of the Kalamas' called Kesaputta.

The Kalamas of Kesaputta thought: "It is very good indeed to see Awakened Ones such as these." And so they went up to where Buddha was. Having seated themselves to one side, the Kalamas of Kesaputta said this to Buddha:

"There are, sir, many different teachers that come to Kesaputta. They illustrate and illuminate their own doctrines, but the doctrines of others they put down, revile, disparage and cripple. For us, sir, uncertainty arises, and doubts arise concerning them: Who indeed of these venerable teachers speaks truly, who speaks falsely?"

"It is indeed fitting, Kalamas, to be uncertain, it is fitting to doubt. For in situations of uncertainty, doubts surely arise. You should decide, Kalamas, not by what you have heard, not by following convention, not by assuming it is so, not by relying on the texts, not because of reasoning, not because of logic, not by thinking about explanations, not by acquiescing to the views that you prefer, not because it appears likely, and certainly not out of respect for a teacher.

"When you would know, Kalamas, for *yourselves,* that 'These things are unhealthy, these things, when entered upon and undertaken, incline toward harm and suffering'—then, Kalamas, you should reject them.

"What do you think, Kalamas? When greed, hatred, or delusion arise within a person, does it arise for their welfare or their harm?"

"For their harm, sir."

"And when a person has become greedy, hateful, or deluded, their mind consumed by this greed, hatred, or delusion, Kalamas, do they kill living creatures, and take what has not been given, and go to another's spouse, and speak what is false, and induce others to undertake what is, for a long time, to their harm and suffering?"

"This is true, sir."

"And what do you think, Kalamas? Are these things healthy or unhealthy?"

"Unhealthy, sir."

"And when entered upon and undertaken, do they incline toward harm and suffering or don't they?"

"We agree, sir, that they do."

"But when you would know, Kalamas, for *yourselves,* that 'These things are healthy, these things, when entered upon and undertaken, incline toward welfare and happiness'—then, Kalamas, having come to them you should stay with them.

"What do you think, Kalamas? When nongreed, nonhatred, or nondelusion arise within a person, does it arise for their welfare or their harm?"

"For their welfare, sir."

"And when a person has not become greedy, hateful, or deluded, their mind not consumed by this greed, hatred, or delusion, Kalamas, do they not kill living creatures, and not take what has not been given, and not go to another's spouse, and not speak what is false, and induce others to undertake what is, for a long time, to their welfare and happiness?"

"This is true, sir."

"And what do you think, Kalamas? Are these things healthy or unhealthy?"

"Healthy, sir."

"And when entered upon and undertaken, do they incline toward welfare and happiness or don't they?"

"We agree, sir, that they do."

"That person, Kalamas, who is a follower of the noble path is thus free of wanting, free of harming, and without confusion. Clearly conscious and mindful, he or she abides having suffused the first direction, then the second, then the third and fourth—and so above, below and across, everywhere and in every way—with a mind dedicated to loving kindness, compassion, good will, and equanimity that is abundant, expansive, immeasurable, kindly, and free of harming.

"And so, Kalamas, the follower of the noble path whose mind is thus kindly and free of harming—their mind is not defiled, but is purified."

(adapted from the *Anguttara Nikaya*,
translated by Andy Olendzki)

The Buddha said: "If outsiders speak against me, the Teaching or the Order, you should not be angry for that would prevent your own self-conquest. Similarly if they praise us. But you should find out what is false or true, and acknowledge the fact. And even in praise it is only of trifling matters that an unconverted man might speak of me."

(from *Digha Nikaya,* translated by C. A. F. Rhys Davids)

Someone who is about to admonish another must realize within himself five qualities before doing so [that he may be able to say], thus:

"In due season will I speak, not out of season. In truth will I speak, not in falsehood. Gently will I speak, not harshly. To his profit will I speak, not to his loss. With kindly intent will I speak, not in anger."

(from the *Vinaya Pitaka,* translated by F. S. Woodward)

RIGHT SPEECH

ABSTAINING FROM LYING

Herein someone avoids lying and abstains from it. One speaks the truth, is devoted to the truth, reliable, worthy of confidence, not a deceiver of men. Being at a meeting, or among people, or in the midst of his relatives, or in a society, or in the king's court, and called upon and asked as witness to tell what one knows, one answers, if one knows nothing: "I know nothing," and if one knows, one answers: "I know"; if one has seen nothing, one answers: "I have seen nothing," and if one has seen, one answers: "I have seen." Thus one never knowingly speaks a lie, either for the sake of one's own advantage, or for the sake of another person's advantage, or for the sake of any advantage whatsoever.

Abstaining from Tale-Bearing

One avoids tale-bearing and abstains from it. What one has heard here, one does not repeat there, so as to cause dissension there; and what one has heard there, one does not repeat here, so as to cause dissension here. Thus one unites those that are divided; and those that are united, one encourages. Concord gladdens one, one delights and rejoices in concord; and it is concord that one spreads by one's words.

Abstaining from Harsh Language

One avoids harsh language, and abstains from it. One speaks such words as are gentle, soothing to the ear, loving, such words as go to the heart, and are courteous, friendly, and agreeable to many.

Abstaining from Vain Talk

One avoids vain talk, and abstains from it. One speaks at the right time, in accordance with facts, speaks what is useful, speaks of the law and the discipline; one's speech is like a treasure, uttered at the right moment, accompanied by arguments, moderate and full of sense.

This is called Right Speech.

(adapted from the *Anguttara Nikaya,*
translated by Nyanatiloka)

"None of the means employed to acquire religious merit, O monks, has a sixteenth part of the value of loving-kindness. Loving-kindness, which is freedom of heart, absorbs them all; it glows, it shines, it blazes forth.

"And in the same way, O monks, as the light of all the stars has not a sixteenth part of the value of the moonlight, but the moonlight absorbs it and glows and shines and blazes forth: in the same way, O monks, none of the means employed to acquire religious merit has a sixteenth part of the value of loving-kindness. Loving-kindness, which is freedom of heart, absorbs them; it glows, it shines, it blazes forth.

"And in the same way, O monks, as at the end of the rainy season, the sun, rising into the clear and cloudless sky, banishes all the dark spaces and glows and shines and blazes forth: in the same way again, as at night's end the morning star glows and shines and blazes forth: so, O monks, none of the means employed to acquire religious merit has a sixteenth part of the value of loving-kindness. Loving-kindness, which is freedom of heart, absorbs them: it glows, it shines, it blazes forth."

(adapted from the *Itivuttaka*,
translated by Justin H. Moore)

A man buries a treasure in a deep pit, thinking: "It will be useful in time of need, or if the king is displeased with me, or if I am robbed or fall into debt, or if food is scarce, or bad luck befalls me."

But all this treasure may not profit the owner at all, for he may forget where he has hidden it, or goblins may steal it, or his enemies or even his kinsmen may take it when he is careless.

But by charity, goodness, restraint, and self-control man and woman alike can store up a well-hidden treasure—a treasure which cannot be given to others and which robbers cannot steal. A wise person should do good—that is the treasure which will not leave one.

(adapted from the *Khuddhaka Patha*, translated by A. L. Basham)

THE FIVE PRECEPTS

1. For the purpose of training I vow to refrain from taking life.
2. For the purpose of training I vow to refrain from taking what is not given.
3. For the purpose of training I vow to refrain from sexual misconduct.
4. For the purpose of training I vow to refrain from false speech.
5. For the purpose of training I vow to refrain from intoxicants which lead to carelessness.

These Five Precepts are a vehicle of happiness, a vehicle of good fortune, a vehicle for liberation. Let our virtue therefore be purified and shine forth.

(translated by Gil Fronsdal)

As long as the followers of the way hold regular and frequent assemblies, they may be expected to prosper and not decline. As long as they meet in harmony, break up in harmony, and carry on their business in harmony, they may be expected to prosper and not decline. As long as they do not authorize what has not been authorized already, and do not abolish what has been authorized, but proceed according to what has been authorized by the rules of training; as long as they honor, respect, revere and salute the elders of long standing who are long ordained, fathers and leaders of the order; as long as they do not fall prey to desires which arise in them and lead to rebirth; as long as they are devoted to forest lodgings; as long as they preserve their personal mindfulness, so that in future the good among their companions will come to them, and those who have already come will feel at ease with them; as long as the followers of the way hold to these seven things and are seen to do so, they may be expected to prosper and not decline.

(from the *Mahaparinibbana Sutta,*
translated by Maurice Walshe)

I heard these words of the Buddha one time when the Lord was staying at the monastery in the Jeta Grove, in the town of Sravasti. He called all the monks to him and instructed them, "Monks!"

And the monks replied, "We are here."

The Blessed One taught, "I will teach you what is meant by 'knowing the better way to live alone.' I will begin with an outline of the teaching, and then I will give a detailed explanation. Monks, please listen carefully."

"Blessed One, we are listening."

The Buddha taught:

"Do not pursue the past.
Do not lose yourself in the future.
The past no longer is.
The future has not yet come.
Looking deeply at life as it is

in the very here and now,
the practitioner dwells
in stability and freedom.
We must be diligent today.
To wait until tomorrow is too late.
Death comes unexpectedly.
How can we bargain with it?
The sage calls a person who knows
how to dwell in mindfulness
night and day
'one who knows
the better way to live alone.' "

(adapted from the *Bhaddekaratta Sutta*,
translated by Thich Nhat Hanh)

"This I do now declare, after investigation there is nothing among the doctrines that such a one as I would embrace. Seeing misery in philosophical views, without adopting any of them, searching for truth I saw 'inward peace.'

"Not by any philosophical opinion, not by tradition, not by knowledge, not by virtue and holy works can anyone say that purity exists; nor by absence of philosophical opinion, by absence of tradition, by absence of knowledge, by absence of virtue and holy works either; having abandoned these without adopting anything else, let one, calm and independent, not desire any resting place.'

"One who thinks oneself equal to others, or distinguished, or low, for that very reason disputes; but one who is unmoved under those three conditions, for that person the notions 'equal' and 'distinguished' do not exist.

"The Sage for whom the notions 'equal' and 'unequal' do not exist, would he say, 'This is true'? Or with whom should he dispute, saying, 'This is false'? With whom should he enter into dispute?

"An accomplished person does not by a philosophical view, or by thinking become arrogant, for he is not of that sort; not by holy works, nor by tradition is he to be led, he is not led into any of the resting places of the mind.

"For one who is free from views there are no ties, for one who is delivered by understanding there are no follies; but those who grasped after views and philosophical opinions, they wander about in the world annoying people."

(adapted from the *Sutta-nipata,*
translated by V. Fausböll)

Do not form views in the world through either knowledge, virtuous conduct, or religious observances; likewise, avoid thinking of oneself as being either superior, inferior, or equal to others.

The wise let go of the 'self' and being free of attachments they depend not on knowledge. Nor do they dispute opinions or settle into any view.

For those who have no wishes for either extremes of becoming or non-becoming, here or in another existence, there is no settling into the views held by others.

Nor do they form the least notion in regard to views seen, heard, or thought out. How could one influence those wise ones who do not grasp at any views.

(from the *Sutta-nipata*, translated by Gil Fronsdal)

"The results of karma cannot be known by thought, and so should not be speculated about. Thus thinking, one would come to distraction and distress.

"Therefore, Ananda, do not be the judge of people; do not make assumptions about others. A person is destroyed by holding judgements about others."

(from the *Anguttara Nikaya*,
translated by F. L. Woodward
and E. M. Hare)

The whole world we travel with our
   thoughts,
Finding nowhere anyone as precious as
   one's own self.
Since each and every person is so
   precious to themselves
Let the self-respecting harm no other
   being.

(from the *Samyutta Nikaya,*
translated by Gil Fronsdal)

Therefore, Ananda, be ye lamps unto yourselves, be ye a refuge to yourselves. Betake yourselves to no external refuge. Hold fast to the Truth as a lamp; hold fast to the Truth as a refuge. Look not for a refuge in anyone beside yourselves. And those, Ananda, who either now or after I am dead shall be a lamp unto themselves, shall betake themselves to no external refuge, but holding fast to the Truth as their lamp, and holding fast to the Truth as their refuge, shall not look for refuge to anyone beside themselves—it is they who shall reach the very topmost Height. But they must be anxious to learn.

(from the *Mahaparinibbana Sutta*, translated by T. W. Rhys-Davids)

Then the Buddha said to his monks, walk over the earth for the blessing of many, for the happiness of many, out of compassion for the world, for the welfare and the blessing and the happiness of gods and men.

(from the *Vinaya Pitaka*,
translated by Geoffrey Parrinder)

By the blessings that have arisen from
    my practice, may my Venerable
    Preceptors,
And Teachers who have helped me,
    Mother, Father and relatives,
King and Queen, worldly powers,
    virtuous human beings,
The Supreme Beings, Demons and
    High Gods, the guardian deities of
    the world, celestial beings,
The Lord of Death; people—friendly,
    indifferent and hostile—
May all beings be well! May the skillful
    deeds done by me,
Bring you three-fold bliss. May this
    quickly bring you to the Deathless.
By this act of goodness and through
    the act of sharing,
May I likewise attain the cutting-off of
    craving and clinging.

Whatever faults I have until I attain
 liberation,
May they quickly perish. Wherever I
 am born, may there be
An upright mind, mindfulness and
 wisdom, austerity and vigor.
May harmful influences not weaken my
 efforts.
The Buddha is the unexcelled
 protector, the Dharma is the
 supreme protection,
Peerless is the "Silent Buddha," the
 Sangha is my true refuge.
By the power of these Supreme Ones,
 may I rise above all ignorance.

(from *Reflections on Sharing Blessings,*
translated by the residents of the
Amaravati Buddhist Centre)

As a blind man feels when he finds a pearl in a dustbin, so am I amazed by the miracle of awakening rising in my consciousness. It is the nectar of immortality that delivers us from death, the treasure that lifts us above poverty into the wealth of giving to life, the tree that gives shade to us when we roam about scorched by life, the bridge that takes us across the stormy river of life, the cool moon of compassion that calms our mind when it is agitated, the sun that dispels darkness, the butter made from the milk of kindness by churning it with the dharma. It is a feast of joy to which all are invited.

(adapted from the *Bodhicharyavatara* by Shantideva, adapted by Eknath Easwaran)

All things conditioned are instable,
      impermanent,
   Fragile in essence, as an unbaked
      pot,
Like something borrowed, or a city
      founded on sand,
   They last a short while only.

They are inevitably destroyed,
   Like plaster washed off in the rains,
Like the sandy bank of a river—
   They are conditioned, and their
      true nature is frail.

They are like the flame of a lamp,
   Which rises suddenly and as soon
      goes out.
They have no power of endurance, like
   the wind

Or like foam, unsubstantial,
    essentially feeble.

The sage knows the beginning and end
    Of consciousness, its production
        and passing away—
The sage knows that it came from
        nowhere and returns to nowhere,
And is empty of reality, like a
        conjuring trick.

The sage knows what is true reality,
    And sees all conditioned things as
        empty and powerless.

(adapted from the *Lalitavistara*,
translated by A. L. Basham)

THE HEART SUTRA

Thus have I heard at one time. The Buddha dwelt at Vulture Peak together with a sangha of one hundred thousand monks and nuns, and seventy thousand bodhisattvas. At that time the bodhisattva Avolokitesvara arose from her seat among the assembly and went up to the Buddha. Facing him she joined her palms together and bowed respectfully. With reverence she said, "I wish to explain for this assembly the bodhisattva's Heart of Perfect Wisdom which is the Universal Womb of Wisdom."

Then the Buddha said, "Excellent, excellent, Great Compassionate One!"

Then Avolokitesvara entered into her meditation and coursing in Perfect Wisdom observed that all five aggregates are empty of own-nature. Arising from her meditation she said:

"The nature of form is empty, emptiness is form. Form is not different from emptiness, emptiness is not different from form. That which is form is empty, that which is emptiness is form. Feelings, perceptions, mental formations and consciousness are also like this. The nature of consciousness is empty, emptiness is consciousness. Consciousness is not different from emptiness, emptiness is not different from consciousness. That which is consciousness is empty, that which is emptiness is consciousness.

"These dharmas are marked with emptiness, neither arising nor ceasing, neither tainted nor pure, neither increasing nor decreasing. Therefore in emptiness there is no form, no feelings, no perceptions, no mental formations, no consciousness, no eye, ear, nose, taste, or touch; no realm of eyes and so on up to no realm of mind-consciousness; no ignorance and no extinction of ignorance, and so on up to no old age and death and also no extinction of old age and death; no suffering, no origin of suffering, no end to suffering, no path, no wisdom and also no attainment.

"With nothing to attain the bodhisattvas depend on Perfect Wisdom and their minds are without any hindrance. Without any hindrance no fears exist. Far removed from perverted thought they are awake. All the Buddhas in the past, present and future depend on Perfect Wisdom in attaining their unsurpassed complete and perfect awakening.

"Therefore, know the Perfection of Wisdom is the great mantra, is the bright mantra, is the unsurpassed mantra, is the unequaled mantra that can remove all suffering, and is true not false.

"Therefore proclaim the Perfect Wisdom mantra. Proclaim the mantra that says,

"GATE, GATE, PARAGATE, PARASAMGATE,
BODHI, SVAHA!"

(*The Heart Sutra,* translated by Gil Fronsdal)

This triple world resembles a net, or water in a mirage that is agitated; it is like a dream, *maya*; and by thus regarding it one is emancipated.

Like a mirage in the springtime, the mind is found bewildered; animals imagine water but there is no reality to it.

There is here nothing but thought construction, it is like an image in the air; when they thus understand all, there is nothing to know.

Eternity and non-eternity; oneness, too, bothness and not-bothness as well: these are discriminated by the ignorant who are confused in mind and bound up by errors since beginningless time.

In a mirror, in water, in an eye, in a vessel, and on a gem, images are seen; but in them there are no realities anywhere to take hold of.

(adapted from the *Lankavatara Sutra,* translated by D. T. Suzuki)

Thereupon, a certain goddess who lived in that house, having heard this teaching of the Dharma of the great heroic bodhisattvas, and being delighted, pleased, and overjoyed, manifested herself in a material body and showered the great spiritual heroes, the bodhisattvas, and the great disciples with heavenly flowers. When the flowers fell on the bodies of the bodhisattvas, they fell off on the floor, but when they fell on the bodies of the great disciples, they stuck to them and did not fall. The great disciples shook the flowers and even tried to use their magical powers, but still the flowers would not shake off. Then, the goddess said to the venerable Śāriputra, "Reverend Śāriputra, why do you shake these flowers?"

Śāriputra replied, "Goddess, these flowers are not proper for religious persons and so we are trying to shake them off."

The goddess said, "Do not say that, reverend Śāriputra. Why? These flowers are proper indeed! Why? Such flowers have neither constructual thought nor discrimination. But the elder Śāriputra has both constructual thought and discrimination.

"Reverend Śāriputra, impropriety for one who has renounced the world for the discipline of the rightly taught Dharma consists of constructual thought and discrimination, yet the elders are full of such thoughts. One who is without such thoughts is always proper.

"Reverend Śāriputra, see how these flowers do not stick to the bodies of these great spiritual heroes, the bodhisattvas! This is because they have eliminated constructual thoughts and discriminations.

"For example, evil spirits have power

over fearful men but cannot disturb the fearless. Likewise, those intimidated by fear of the world are in the power of forms, sounds, smells, tastes, and textures, which do not disturb those who are free from fear of the passions inherent in the constructive world. Thus, these flowers stick to the bodies of those who have not eliminated their instincts for the passions and do not stick to the bodies of those who have eliminated their instincts. Therefore, the flowers do not stick to the bodies of these bodhisattvas, who have abandoned all instincts."

Śāriputra asked: Goddess, what prevents you from transforming yourself out of your female state?

The goddess replied: Although I have sought my "female state" for these twelve years, I have not yet found it. Reverend Śāriputra, if a magician were to incarnate a woman by magic, would you ask her,

"What prevents you from transforming yourself out of your female state?"

Śāriputra: No! Such a woman would not really exist, so what would there be to transform?

Goddess: Just so, reverend Śāriputra, all things do not really exist. Now, would you think, "What prevents one whose nature is that of a magical incarnation from transforming herself out of her female state?"

Thereupon the goddess employed her magical power to cause the elder Śāriputra to appear in her form and to cause herself to appear in his form. Then the goddess, transformed into Śāriputra, said to Śāriputra, transformed into a goddess, "Reverend Śāriputra, what prevents you from transforming yourself out of your female state?"

And Śāriputra, transformed into the goddess, replied, "I no longer appear in the form of a male! My body has changed into the body of a woman! I do not know what to transform!"

The goddess continued, "If the elder could again change out of the female state, then all women could also change out of their female states. All women appear in the form of women in just the same way as the elder appears in the form of a woman. While they are not women in reality, they appear in the form of women. With this in mind, the Buddha said, 'In all things, there is neither male nor female.'"

Then, the goddess released her magical power and each returned to his ordinary form. She then said to him, "Reverend Śāriputra, what have you done with your female form?"

Śāriputra: I neither made it nor did I change it.

Goddess: Just so, all things are neither

made nor changed, and that they are not
made and not changed, that is the teaching
of the Buddha.

(from *The Vimalakirti Sutra*,
translated by Robert A. F. Thurman)

Thus shall ye think of all this fleeting
   world:
A star at dawn, a bubble in a stream;
A flash of lightning in a summer cloud,
A flickering lamp, a phantom, and a
   dream.

(from the *Diamond Sutra,*
translated by A. F. Price)

VERSES ON THE FAITH MIND
by SENG-TSAN, *the third Zen patriarch*

The Great Way is not difficult
for those who have no preferences.
When love and hate are both absent
everything becomes clear and
    undisguised.
Make the smallest distinction however
and heaven and earth are set infinitely
    apart.
If you wish to see the truth
then hold no opinions for or against
    anything.
To set up what you like against what
    you dislike is the disease of the
    mind.
When the deep meaning of things is
    not understood

the mind's essential peace is disturbed
     to no avail.

The Way is perfect like vast space
where nothing is lacking and nothing
     is in excess.
Indeed, it is due to our choosing to
     accept or reject
that we do not see the true nature of
     things.
Live neither in the entanglements of
     outer things,
nor in inner feelings of emptiness.
Be serene in the oneness of things
and such erroneous views will
     disappear by themselves.
When you try to stop activity to
     achieve passivity
your very effort fills you with activity.
As long as you remain in one extreme
     or the other
you will never know Oneness.

TEACHINGS OF THE BUDDHA

Those who do not live in the single
    Way
fail in both activity and passivity,
assertion and denial.
To deny the reality of things
is to miss their reality;
to assert the emptiness of things
is to miss their reality.
The more you talk and think about it,
the further astray you wander from
    the truth.
Stop talking and thinking,
and there is nothing you will not be
    able to know.
To return to the root is to find the
    meaning,
but to pursue appearances is to miss
    the source.
At the moment of inner enlightenment
there is a going beyond appearance
    and emptiness.

The changes that appear to occur in
    the empty world
we call real only because of our
    ignorance.
Do not search for the truth;
only cease to cherish opinions.

Do not remain in the dualistic state
avoid such pursuits carefully.
If there is even a trace
of this and that, of right and wrong,
the Mind-essence will be lost in
    confusion.
Although all dualities come from the
    One,
do not be attached even to this One.

When the mind exists undisturbed in
    the Way,
nothing in the world can offend,

and when a thing can no longer
offend,
it ceases to exist in the old way.

When no discriminating thoughts
arise,
the old mind ceases to exist.
When thought objects vanish,
the thinking-subject vanishes,
as when the mind vanishes, objects
vanish.
Things are objects because of the
subject [mind];
the mind [subject] is such because of
things [object].
Understand the relativity of these two
and the basic reality: the unity of
emptiness.
In this Emptiness the two are
indistinguishable
and each contains in itself the whole
world.

If you do not discriminate between
    coarse and fine
you will not be tempted to prejudice
    and opinion.

To live in the Great Way
is neither easy nor difficult,
but those with limited views
are fearful and irresolute:
the faster they hurry, the slower they
    go,
and clinging [attachment] cannot be
    limited:
even to be attached to the idea of
    enlightenment
is to go astray.
Just let things be in their own way
and there will be neither coming nor
    going.

Obey the nature of things [your own
    nature],

and you will walk freely and
    undisturbed.
When thought is in bondage the truth
    is hidden,
for everything is murky and unclear
and the burdensome practice of
    judging
brings annoyance and weariness.
What benefit can be derived
from distinctions and separations?

If you wish to move in the One Way
do not dislike even the world of senses
    and ideas.
Indeed, to accept them fully
is identical with true Enlightenment.
The wise man strives to no goals
but the foolish man fetters himself.
There is one Dharma, not many;
distinctions arise
from the clinging needs of the
    ignorant.

To seek Mind with the [discriminating]
    mind
is the greatest of all mistakes.

Rest and unrest derive from passion;
with enlightenment there is no liking
    and disliking.
All dualities come from ignorant
    inference.
They are like dreams or flowers in air:
foolish to try to grasp them.
Gain and loss, right and wrong:
such thoughts must finally be
    abolished at once.

If the eye never sleeps,
all dreams will naturally cease.
If the mind makes no discriminations,
the ten thousand things are as they
    are, of single essence.
To understand the mystery of this One
    essence

is to be released from all
    entanglements.
When all things are seen equally
the timeless Self-essence is reached.
No comparisons or analogies are
    possible
in this causeless, relationless state.

Consider movement stationary
and the stationary in motion,
both movement and rest disappear.
When such dualities cease to exist
Oneness itself cannot exist.
To this ultimate finality
no law or description applies.

For the unified mind in accord with
    the Way
All self-centered striving ceases.
Doubts and irresolutions vanish
and life in true faith is possible.

With a single stroke we are free from
    bondage;
nothing clings to us and we hold to
    nothing.
All is empty, clear, self-illuminating,
with no exertion of the mind's power.
Here thought, feeling, knowledge, and
    imagination are of no value.
In this world of Suchness
there is neither self nor other-than-
    self.

To come directly into harmony with
    this reality
just simply say when doubt arises,
    "Not two."
In this "not two" nothing is separate,
nothing is excluded.
No matter when or where,
enlightenment means entering this
    truth.

And this truth is beyond extension or
    diminution in time or space;
in it a single thought is ten thousand
    years.

Emptiness here, Emptiness there,
but the infinite universe stands
always before your eyes.
Infinitely large and infinitely small;
no difference, for definitions have
    vanished
and no boundaries are seen.
So too with Being and non-Being.
Don't waste time in doubts and
    arguments
that have nothing to do with this.

One thing, all things:
move among and intermingle,
without distinction.
To live in this realization

is to be without anxiety about non-
    perfection.
To live in this faith is the road to non-
    duality.
Because the non-dual is one with the
    trusting mind.

Words!
The Way is beyond language,
for in it there is
    no yesterday
    no tomorrow
    no today.

(translated by Richard B. Clarke)

THE PRACTICE
OF MEDITATION
by ZEN MASTER DOGEN

Truth is perfect and complete in itself. It is not something newly discovered; it has always existed.

Truth is not far away; it is ever present. It is not something to be attained since not one of your steps leads away from it.

Do not follow the ideas of others, but learn to listen to the voice within yourself. Your body and mind will become clear and you will realize the unity of all things.

The slightest movement of your dualistic thought will prevent you from entering the palace of meditation and wisdom.

The Buddha meditated for six years, Bodhidharma for nine. The practice of meditation is not a method for the attainment of realization—it is enlightenment itself.

Your search among books, word upon word, may lead you to the depths of knowledge, but it is not the way to receive the reflection of your true self.

When you have thrown off your ideas as to mind and body, the original truth will fully appear. Zen is simply the expression of truth; therefore longing and striving are not the true attitudes of Zen.

To actualize the blessedness of meditation you should practice with pure intention and firm determination. Your meditation room should be clean and quiet. Do not dwell in thoughts of good or bad. Just relax and forget that you are meditating. Do not desire realization since that thought will keep you confused.

Sit on a cushion in a manner as comfortable as possible, wearing loose clothing. Hold your body straight without leaning to the left or the right, forward or backward. Your ears should be in line with your shoulders, and your nose in a straight line with your navel. Keep your tongue at the roof of your mouth and close your lips. Keep your eyes slightly open, and breathe through your nostrils.

Before you begin meditation take several slow, deep breaths. Hold your body erect, allowing your breathing to become normal again. Many thoughts will crowd into your mind, ignore them, letting them go. If they persist be aware of them with the awareness which does not think. In other words, think non-thinking.

Zen meditation is not physical culture, nor is it a method to gain something material. It is peacefulness and blessedness itself. It is the actualization of truth and wisdom.

In your meditation you yourself are the

mirror reflecting the solution of your problems. The human mind has absolute freedom within its true nature. You can attain your freedom intuitively. Do not work for freedom, rather allow the practice itself to be liberation.

When you wish to rest, move your body slowly and stand up quietly. Practice this meditation in the morning or in the evening, or at any leisure time during the day. You will soon realize that your mental burdens are dropping away one by one, and that you are gaining an intuitive power hitherto unnoticed.

There are thousands upon thousands of students who have practiced meditation and obtained its fruits. Do not doubt its possibilities because of the simplicity of the method. If you cannot find the truth right where you are, where else do you expect to find it?

Life is short and no one knows what the

next moment will bring. Open your mind while you have the opportunity, thereby gaining the treasures of wisdom, which in turn you can share abundantly with others, bringing them happiness.

(adapted from the *Fukanzazengi*, translated by Senzaki and McCandless)

ACTUALIZING THE
FUNDAMENTAL POINT
by ZEN MASTER DOGEN

As all things are buddha-dharma, there is delusion and realization, practice, and birth and death, and there are buddhas and sentient beings.

As the myriad things are without an abiding self, there is no delusion, no realization, no buddha, no sentient being, no birth and death.

The buddha way is, basically, leaping clear of the many and the one; thus there are birth and death, delusion and realization, sentient beings and buddhas.

Yet in attachment blossoms fall, and in aversion weeds spread.

To carry yourself forward and experience myriad things is delusion. That myriad things come forth and experience themselves is awakening.

Those who have great realization of delusion are buddhas; those who are greatly deluded about realization are sentient beings. Further, there are those who continue realizing beyond realization, who are in delusion throughout delusion.

When buddhas are truly buddhas they do not necessarily notice that they are buddhas. However, they are actualized buddhas, who go on actualizing buddhas.

To study the buddha way is to study the self. To study the self is to forget the self. To forget the self is to be actualized by myriad things. When actualized by myriad things, your body and mind as well as the bodies and minds of others drop away. No trace of realization remains, and this no-trace continues endlessly.

When you ride in a boat and watch the shore, you might assume that the shore is moving. But when you keep your eyes closely on the boat, you can see that the boat moves. Similarly, if you examine myriad things with a confused body and mind you might suppose that your mind and nature are permanent. When you practice intimately and return to where you are, it will be clear that nothing at all has unchanging self.

Firewood becomes ash, and it does not become firewood again. Yet, do not suppose that the ash is future and the firewood past. You should understand that firewood is firewood, which fully includes past and future. Ash is ash, which fully includes future and past. Just as firewood does not become firewood again after it is ash, you do not return to birth after death.

This being so, it is an established way in

buddha-dharma to deny that birth turns into death. Accordingly, birth is understood as no-birth. It is an unshakable teaching in Buddha's discourse that death does not turn into birth. Accordingly, death is understood as no-death.

Birth is an expression complete this moment. Death is an expression complete this moment. They are like winter and spring. You do not call winter the beginning of spring, nor summer the end of spring.

Enlightenment is like the moon reflected on the water. The moon does not get wet, nor is the water broken. Although its light is wide and great, the moon is reflected even in a puddle an inch wide. The whole moon and the entire sky are reflected in dewdrops on the grass, or even in one drop of water.

Enlightenment does not divide you, just

as the moon does not break the water. You cannot hinder enlightenment, just as a drop of water does not hinder the moon in the sky.

The depth of the drop is the height of the moon. Each reflection, however long or short its duration, manifests the vastness of the dewdrop, and realizes the limitlessness of the moonlight in the sky.

When dharma does not fill your whole body and mind, you think it is already sufficient. When dharma fills your body and mind, you understand that something is missing.

For example, when you sail out in a boat to the middle of an ocean where no land is in sight, and view the four directions, the ocean looks circular, and does not look any other way. But the ocean is neither round nor square; its features are infinite in variety. It is like a palace. It is like a jewel. It only looks circular as far as you can see at that time. All things are like this.

Though there are many features in the dusty world and the world beyond conditions, you see and understand only what your eye of practice can reach. In order to learn the nature of the myriad things, you must know that although they may look round or square, the other features of oceans and mountains are infinite in variety; whole worlds are there. It is so not only around you, but also directly beneath your feet, or in a drop of water.

A fish swims in the ocean, and no matter how far it swims there is no end to the water. A bird flies in the sky, and no matter how far it flies there is no end to the air. However, the fish and the bird have never left their elements. When their activity is large their field is large. When their need is small their field is small. Thus, each of them totally covers its full range, and each of them totally experiences its realm. If the bird leaves the air it will die at once. If the fish leaves the water it will die at once.

Know that water is life and air is life. The bird is life and the fish is life. Life must be the bird and life must be the fish.

It is possible to illustrate this with more analogies. Practice, enlightenment, and people are like this.

Now if a bird or a fish tries to reach the end of its element before moving in it, this bird or this fish will not find its way or its place. When you find your place where you are, practice occurs, actualizing the fundamental point. When you find your way at this moment, practice occurs, actualizing the fundamental point; for the place, the way, is neither large nor small, neither yours nor others'. The place, the way, has not carried over from the past, and it is not merely arising now.

Accordingly, in the practice-enlightenment of the buddha way, meeting one thing is mastering it—doing one practice is practicing completely.

Zen master Baoche of Mt. Mayu was fanning himself. A monk approached and said, "Master, the nature of wind is permanent and there is no place it does not reach. Why, then, do you fan yourself?"

"Although you understand that the nature of the wind is permanent," Baoche replied, "you do not understand the meaning of its reaching everywhere."

"What is the meaning of its reaching everywhere?" asked the monk again. The master just kept fanning himself. The monk bowed deeply.

The actualization of the buddha-dharma, the vital path of its correct transmission, is like this. If you say that you do not need to fan yourself because the nature of wind is permanent and you can have wind without fanning, you will understand neither permanence nor the nature of wind. The nature of wind is permanent; because of that, the wind of the buddha's house brings forth the gold of the earth and makes fragrant the cream of the long river.

(adapted from the *Genjo Koan*,
translated by Robert Aitken
and Kazuaki Tanahashi)

THE SONG OF MAHAMUDRA*
by TILOPA

Mahamudra is beyond all words and
   symbols,
But for you, Naropa, earnest and loyal,
   must this be said.

The Void needs no reliance;
   Mahamudra rests on naught.
Without making an effort, but
   remaining natural,
One can break the yoke thus gaining
   liberation.

If one looks for naught when staring
   into space;

---

*Mahamudra is the practice and teaching that leads to the
realization of One Mind.

If with the mind one then observes the
    mind;
One destroys distinctions and reaches
    Buddhahood.

The clouds that wander through the
    sky have no roots, no home,
Nor do the distinctive thoughts
    floating through the mind.
Once the Self-mind is seen,
    Discrimination stops.

In space, shapes and colors form
But neither by black nor white is space
    tinged.
From the Self-mind all things emerge;
The Mind by virtues and by vices is
    not stained.

The darkness of ages cannot shroud
    the glowing sun;

The long eons of Samsara ne'er can
   hide the Mind's brilliant Light.

Though words are spoken to explain
   the Void, the Void as such can never
   be expressed. Though we say "the
   Mind is a bright light," it is beyond
   all words and symbols. Although the
   Mind is void in essence, all things it
   embraces and contains.

Do naught with the body but relax;
Shut firm the mouth and silent remain;
Empty your mind and think of naught.
Like a hollow bamboo rest at ease
   your body.
Giving not nor taking, put your mind
   at rest.
Mahamudra is like a mind that clings
   to naught.
Thus practicing, in time you will reach
   Buddhahood.

The practice of Mantra and
  Perfections, instruction in the Sutras
  and Precepts, and teaching from the
  Schools and Scriptures will not
  bring realization of the Innate
  Truth.
For if the mind when filled with some
  desire should seek a goal, it only
  hides the Light.

One who keeps Tantric Precepts yet
  discriminates, betrays the vows of
  Awakening,
Cease all activity; abandon all desire;
  let thoughts rise and fall as they will
  like the ocean waves.
One who never harms the Non-abiding
  nor the Principles of non-
  distinction, upholds the Tantric
  Precepts.

He who abandons craving and clings
    not to this or that,
Perceives the real meaning given in the
    Scriptures.

In Mahamudra all one's sins are
    burned; in Mahamudra one is
    released from the prison of this
    world. This is the Dharma's
    supreme torch. Those who
    disbelieve it are fools who ever
    wallow in misery and sorrow.

To strive for Liberation one should rely
    on a Guru. When your mind
    receives the Guru's blessing
    emancipation is at hand.

Alas, all things in this world are
    meaningless; they are but sorrow's
    seeds. Small teachings lead to acts.

One should only follow teachings
that are great.

To transcend duality is the Kingly
View; to conquer distractions is the
Royal Practice; the Path of No-
practice is the Way of Buddhas. One
who treads that Path reaches
Buddhahood.

Transient is this world; like phantoms
and dreams,
Substance it has none. Grasp not the
world nor your kin;
Cut the strings of lust and hatred;
meditate in woods and mountains.
If without effort you remain loosely in
the "natural state," soon
Mahamudra you will win and attain
the Non-attainment.

Cut the root of a tree and the leaves
    will wither;
Cut the root of your mind and
    Samsara falls.

The light of any lamp dispels in a
    moment the darkness of long eons;
The strong light of the mind in but a
    flash will burn the veil of ignorance.

Whoever clings to mind sees not the
    truth of what's beyond the mind.
Whoever strives to practice Dharma
    finds not the truth of Beyond-
    practice.
One should cut cleanly through the
    root of mind and stare naked.
One should thus break away from all
    distinctions and remain at ease.

One should not give or take but
    remain natural, for Mahamudra is
    beyond all acceptance and rejection.
Since the consciousness is not born, no
    one can obstruct or soil it;
Staying in the "Unborn" realm all
    appearances will dissolve into the
    ultimate Dharma.
All self-will and pride will vanish into
    naught.

The supreme Understanding
    transcends all this and that.
The supreme Action embraces great
    resourcefulness without attachment.
The supreme Accomplishment is to
    realize immanence without hope.

At first a yogi feels his mind is
    tumbling like a waterfall;
In mid-course, like the Ganges, it
    flows on slow and gentle;
In the end, it is a great vast ocean,
Where the Lights of Child and Mother
    merge in one.

(adapted from the translation
by Garma C. C. Chang)

TIBETAN BOOK OF
THE GREAT LIBERATION

There being really no duality, separation
is untrue. Until duality is transcended and
at-one-ment realized, Enlightenment cannot be attained. The whole Samsara and
Nirvana, as an inseparable unity, are one's
mind.

Owing to worldly beliefs, which he is
free to accept or reject, a person wanders
in Samsara. Therefore, practicing the
Dharma, freed from every attachment,
grasp the whole essence of these teachings.

Although the One Mind is, it has not
existence.

When one seeks one's mind in its true
state, it is found to be quite intelligible,
although invisible. In its true state, mind is

naked, immaculate; not made of anything, being of the Voidness; clear, vacuous, without duality, transparent, timeless, uncompounded, unimpeded, colorless; not realizable as a separate thing, but as the unity of all things, yet not composed of them; of one taste, and transcendent over differentiation.

The One Mind being verily of the Voidness and without any foundation, one's mind is likewise as vacuous as the sky. To know whether this is so or not, look within thine own mind. Being merely a flux of instability like the air of the firmament, objective appearances are without power to fascinate and fetter. To know whether this be so or not, look within thine own mind. Arising of themselves and being naturally free like the clouds in the sky, all external appearances verily fade away into their own respective places. To know whether this be so or not, look within thine own mind. The Dharma being nowhere save in the mind, there is no other place of meditation than the mind. The Dharma being nowhere save in the mind, there is no other doctrine to be taught or practiced elsewhere. The Dharma being nowhere save in the mind, there is no other place of truth for the observance of a vow. The Dharma being nowhere save in the mind, there is no Dharma elsewhere whereby Liberation may be attained. Again and again look within thine own mind.

When looking outward into the vacuity of space, there is no place to be found where the mind is shining. When looking inward into one's own mind in search of the shining, there is to be found no thing that shines.

One's own mind is transparent, without quality. Being void of quality it is comparable to a cloudless sky.

The state of mind transcendent over all dualities brings Liberation.

Again and again, look within thine own mind.

(translated by W. Y. Evans-Wentz)

TIBETAN BOOK OF THE DEAD

Remember the clear light, the pure clear white light from which everything in the universe comes, to which everything in the universe returns; the original nature of your own mind. The natural state of the universe unmanifest.

Let go into the clear light, trust it, merge with it. It is your own true nature, it is home.

The visions you experience exist within your consciousness; the forms they take are determined by your past attachments, your past desires, your past fears, your past karma.

These visions have no reality outside your consciousness. No matter how frightening some of them may seem they cannot hurt you. Just watch them pass through your consciousness. They will all pass in time. No need to become involved with them; no need to become attracted to the beautiful visions; no need to be repulsed by the frightening ones. No need to be seduced or excited by the sexual ones. No need to be attached to them at all.

Just let them pass. If you become involved with these visions, you may have to wander for a long time confused. Just let them pass through your consciousness like clouds passing through an empty sky.

Fundamentally they have no more reality than this.

Remember these teachings, remember the clear light, the pure bright shining white light of your own nature, it is deathless.

If you can look into the visions you can experience and recognize that they are composed of the same pure clear white light as everything else in the universe.

No matter where or how far you wander, the light is only a split second, a half-breath away, it is never too late to recognize the clear light.

(adapted from the translation
by W. Y. Evans-Wentz)

"Followers of the Way, the one right here before your eyes and listening to the Dharma is the person who 'enters fire without being burned, goes into water without being drowned, and plays about in the three deepest hells, as if in a fairground; he enters the world of hungry spirits and dumb animals without being molested by them.'

"Why is this so? Because there is nothing he dislikes. If you love the sacred and dislike the worldly, you will go on floating and sinking in the ocean of birth and death. The passions arise depending on the heart. If the heart is stilled, where then do you seize the passions? Do not tire yourselves by making up discriminations; and quite naturally, of itself, you will find the Way."

(from *Rinzai roku*, translated by Irmgard Schloegl)

"The Bodhisattva comes as neither coming nor going; the Bodhisattva comes as neither moving nor staying, as neither dead nor born, as neither staying nor passing away, as neither departing nor rising, as neither hoping nor getting attached, as neither doing nor reaping the reward, as neither being born nor gone to annihilation, as neither eternal nor bound for death.

"And yet it is in this way that the Bodhisattva comes: he comes where an all-embracing love abides, because he desires to discipline all beings; he comes where there is a great compassionate heart, because he desires to protect all beings against sufferings; he comes where there are deeds of morality, because he desires to be born wherever he can be agreeable; he comes wherever there are great vows to fulfill because of the power of the original vows; he comes out of the miraculous powers because wherever he is sought after he manifests himself to please people; he comes where there is effortlessness because he is never away from the footsteps of all the Buddhas; he comes where there is neither giving nor taking because in his movements mental and physical there is no trace of striving; he comes out of the skillful means born of transcendental knowledge because he is ever in conformity with the mentalities of all beings; he comes where transformations are manifested because all that appears is like a reflection, like a transformed body."

(from *The Flower Ornament Sutra*, translated by D. T. Suzuki)

"Subhuti, someone who has set out in the vehicle of a Bodhisattva should produce a thought in this manner: 'As many beings as there are in the universe of beings, comprehended under the term *beings*—either egg-born, or born from a womb, or moisture-born, or miraculously born; with or without form; with perception, without perception, or with neither perception nor non-perception—as far as any conceivable universe of beings is concerned: all these should by me be led to Nirvana, into that Realm of Nirvana which leaves nothing behind. And yet, although innumerable beings have thus been led to Nirvana, no being at all has been led to Nirvana.' And why? If in a Bodhisattva the perception of a 'being' should take place, he could not be called a 'Bodhi-being.' And why? He is not to be called a Bodhi-being in whom

the perception of a self or a being would
take place, or the perception of a living
soul or a person."

(from the *Diamond Sutra,*
translated by Edward Conze)

Sariputra: "What is the worldly, and what is the supramundane perfection of giving?"

Subhuti: "The worldly perfection of giving consists in this: The Bodhisattva gives liberally to all those who ask, all the while thinking in terms of real things. It occurs to him: 'I give, that one receives, this is the gift. I renounce all my possessions without stint. I act as one who knows the Buddha. I practice the perfection of giving. I, having made this gift into the common property of all beings, dedicate it to supreme enlightenment, and that without apprehending anything. By means of this gift and its fruit may all beings in this very life be at their ease, and may they one day enter Nirvana!' Tied by three ties he gives a gift. Which three? A perception of self, a perception of others, a perception of the gift.

"The supramundane perfection of giving, on the other hand, consists in the threefold purity. What is the threefold purity? Here a Bodhisattva gives a gift, and he does not apprehend a self, nor a recipient, nor a gift; also no reward of his giving. He surrenders that gift to all beings, but he apprehends neither beings nor self. He dedicates that gift to supreme enlightenment, but he does not apprehend any enlightenment. This is called the supramundane perfection of giving."

(from the *Perfection of Wisdom Sutra in 25,000 Lines,* translated by Edward Conze)

THE SUTRA OF HUI-NENG

"Now that you have already taken refuge in the threefold body of Buddha, I shall expound to you the four great vows. Good friends, recite in unison what I say: 'I vow to save all sentient beings everywhere. I vow to cut off all the passions everywhere. I vow to study all the Buddhist teachings everywhere. I vow to achieve the unsurpassed Buddha Way.'

"Learned Audience, all of us have now declared that we vow to deliver an infinite number of sentient beings; but what does it mean? It does not mean that I, Hui-neng, am going to deliver them. And who are these sentient beings within our mind? They are the delusive mind, the deceitful mind, the evil mind, and suchlike minds — all these are sentient beings. Each of them has to deliver itself by means of its own essence of mind. Then the deliverance is genuine.

"Now, what does it mean to deliver oneself by one's own essence of mind? It means the deliverance of the ignorant, the elusive, and the vexatious beings within our mind by means of right views.

"Enlightened by right views, we call
    forth the buddha within us.
When our nature is dominated by the
    three poisonous elements
We are said to be possessed by Mara;
But when right views eliminate from
    our mind these poisonous elements
Mara will be transformed into a real
    buddha.

"When our temperament is such that
    we are no longer the slaves of the
    five sense objects,

And when we have realized the essence
of mind even for one moment only,
then truth is known to us.

"One who is able to realize the truth
within one's own mind
Has sown the seed of buddhahood.

"Hear me, future disciples!
Your time will have been badly wasted
if you neglect to put this teaching
into practice."

"What you should do is to know your
own mind and realize your own buddha-
nature, which neither rests nor moves,
neither becomes nor ceases to be, neither
comes nor goes, neither affirms nor denies,
neither stays nor departs.

Imperturbable and serene, the ideal
  person practices no virtue.
Self-possessed and dispassionate, he
  commits no sin.
Calm and silent, he gives up seeing and
  hearing.
Even and upright, his mind abides
  nowhere."

(adapted from the translations by
Philip Yampolsky and A. F. Price)

Those who are afraid of the sorrow which arises from the round of birth-and-death seek for Nirvana; they do not realize that between birth-and-death and Nirvana there is really no difference at all. They see Nirvana as the absence of all becoming, and the cessation of all contact of sense-organ and sense-object, and they will not understand that it is really only the inner realization of the store of impressions. Hence they teach the three Vehicles, but not the doctrine that nothing truly exists but the mind, in which are no images. Therefore, they do not know the extent of what has been perceived by the minds of past, present, and future Buddhas, and continue in the conviction that the world extends beyond the range of the mind's eye. And so they keep on rolling on the wheel of birth-and-death.

(from *Lankavatara Sutra,* translated by A. L. Basham)

Just understand that birth and death itself is nirvana, and you will neither hate one as being birth and death nor cherish the other as being nirvana. Only then can you be free of birth and death.

This present birth and death is the life of Buddha. If you reject it with distaste, you are thereby losing the life of Buddha. If you abide in it, attaching to birth and death, you also lose the life of Buddha. But do not try to gauge it with your mind or speak it with words. When you simply release and forget both your body and your mind and throw yourself into the house of Buddha, then with no strength needed and no thought expended, freed from birth and death, you become Buddha. Then there can be no obstacle in any person's mind.

There is an extremely easy way to become Buddha. Refraining from all evil, not clinging to birth and death, working in deep compassion for all sentient beings, respecting those over you and pitying those below you, without any detesting or desiring, worrying or lamentation—this is what is called Buddha. Do not search beyond it.

(from "Birth and Death" by Zen Master Dogen, translated by Masao Abe and Norman Waddell)

"Your true nature is something never lost
to you even in moments of delusion, nor is
it gained at the moment of Enlightenment.
It is the Nature of the Suchness. In it is
neither delusion nor right understanding.
It fills the Void everywhere and is intrinsi-
cally of the substance of the One Mind.
How, then, can your mind-created objects
exist outside the Void? The Void is fundamentally without spacial dimensions, passions, activities, delusions or right
understanding. You must clearly understand that in it there are no things, no men
and no Buddhas; for this Void contains not
the smallest hairbreadth of anything that
can be viewed spacially; it depends on
nothing and is attached to nothing. It is all-
pervading, spotless beauty; it is the self-
existent and uncreated Absolute. Then
how can it even be a matter for discussion

that the *real* Buddha has no mouth and preaches no Dharma, or that *real* hearing requires no ears, for who could hear it? Ah, it is a jewel beyond all price.

"This pure Mind, the source of everything, shines forever and on all with the brilliance of its own perfection. But the people of the world do not awake to it, regarding only that which sees, hears, feels and knows as mind. Blinded by their own sight, hearing, feeling and knowing, they do not perceive the spiritual brilliance of the source-substance. If they would only eliminate all conceptual thought in a flash, that source-substance would manifest itself like the sun ascending through the void and illuminating the whole universe without hindrance or bounds. Therefore, if you students of the Way seek to progress through seeing, hearing, feeling and knowing, when you are deprived of your perceptions, your way to Mind will be cut off and you will find nowhere to enter. Only realize that, though real Mind is expressed in these perceptions, it neither forms part of them nor is separate from them. You should not start *reasoning* from these perceptions, nor allow them to give rise to conceptual thought; yet nor should you seek the One Mind apart from them or abandon them in your pursuit of the Dharma. Do not keep them nor abandon them nor dwell in them nor cleave to them. Above, below and around you, all is spontaneously existing, for there is nowhere which is outside the Buddha-Mind."

(from *The Zen Teachings of Huang Po,*
translated by John Blofeld)

"World-honored One! It is as if some man goes to an intimate friend's house, gets drunk, and falls asleep. Meanwhile his friend, having to go forth on official duty, ties a priceless jewel within his garment as a present, and departs. The man, being drunk and asleep, knows nothing of it. On arising he travels onward till he reaches some other country, where for food and clothing he expends much labor and effort, and undergoes exceedingly great hardship, and is content even if he can obtain but little. Later, his friend happens to meet him and speaks thus: 'Tut! Sir, how is it you have come to this for the sake of food and clothing? Wishing you to be in comfort and able to satisfy all your five senses, I formerly in such a year and month and on such a day tied a priceless jewel within your garment. Now as of old it is present there and you in ignorance are slaving and worrying to keep yourself alive. How very stupid! Go you now and exchange that jewel for what you need and do whatever you will, free from all poverty and shortage.' "

(from the *Lotus Sutra*, translated by
Bunno Kato and W. E. Soothill)

SONG OF ZAZEN
by HAKUIN ZENJI

All beings by nature are Buddha,
as ice by nature is water.
Apart from water there is no ice;
apart from beings, no Buddha.

How sad that people ignore the near
and search for truth afar:
like someone in the midst of water
crying out in thirst;
like a child of a wealthy home
wandering among the poor.

Lost on dark paths of ignorance,
we wander through the Six Worlds;
from dark path to dark path—
when shall we be freed from birth and
    death?

Oh, the Zen meditation of the
    Mahayana!
To this the highest praise!
Devotion, repentance, training,
the many perfections—
all have their source in Zen meditation.

Those who try Zen meditation even
    once
wipe away beginningless crimes.
Where are all the dark paths then?
The Pure Land itself is near.

Those who hear this truth even once
and listen with a grateful heart,
treasuring it, revering it,
gain blessings without end.

Much more, those who turn about
and bear witness to self-nature,
self-nature that is no-nature,
go far beyond mere doctrine.

Here effect and cause are the same;
the Way is neither two nor three.
With form that is no-form,
going and coming, we are never astray;
with thought that is no-thought,
even singing and dancing are the voice
    of the Law.

How boundless and free is the sky of
    Awareness!
How bright the full moon of wisdom!
Truly, is anything missing now?
Nirvana is right here, before our eyes;
this very place is the Lotus Land;
this very body, the Buddha.

                    (adapted from the translation
                        by Robert Aitken)

SOURCES

Anguttara Nikaya, pp. 36–37, 87–89: from Nyanapon-
    ika Thera (trans.), *Anguttara Nikaya: Discourses of
    the Buddha, an Anthology* (Kandy, Sri Lanka:
    Buddhist Publication Society, 1975).

Anguttara Nikaya, pp. 53, 109–111: from Nyanatiloka
    (trans.), *The Word of the Buddha* (Kandy, Ceylon:
    Buddhist Publication Society, 1971).

Anguttara Nikaya, pp. 102–106, from Andy Olendzki
    (trans.), *Inquiring Mind.*

Anguttara Nikaya, p. 120: from Kerry Brown and
    Joanne O'Brien (eds.), *The Essential Teachings of
    Buddhism* (London: Rider Books, 1989).

Bhaddekaratta Sutta, pp. 118–119: from Thich Nhat
    Hanh, *Our Appointment with Life* (Berkeley,
    Calif.: Parallax Press, 1990).

"Birth and Death," pp. 198–199: from Masao Abe
    and Norman Waddell (trans.), in *The Eastern
    Buddhist,* vol. 5, no. 1 (May, 1972).

Bodhicharyavatara, p. 129: from Eknath Easwaran, *God
    Makes the Rivers to Flow* (Tomales, Calif.: Nilgiri
    Press, n.d.).

Buddhist Parables, pp. 48–52: from E. W. Burlingame (trans.), *Buddhist Parables* (New Haven, Conn.: Yale University Press, 1922).

Dhammapada, pp. 1, 4–5, 10, 11, 17–18, 19–20, 28, 46–47, 61–62, 65, 69, 78, 96: from Thomas Byrom (trans.), *The Dhammapada: The Sayings of the Buddha* (New York: Alfred A. Knopf, 1976).

Dhammapada, pp. 32–34: from Nyanamoli Thera (ed.), *The Life of the Buddha* (Kandy, Sri Lanka: Buddhist Publication Society, 1978).

Diamond Sutra, p. 143: from A. F. Price and Wong Mou-lam (trans.), *The Diamond Sutra and the Sutra of Hui-neng* (Boston: Shambhala Publications, 1990).

Diamond Sutra, pp. 189–190: from Edward Conze (trans.), *Buddhist Wisdom Books* (London: George Allen & Unwin, 1958).

Digha Nikaya, p. 9: from Maurice Walshe (trans.), *Thus Have I Heard* (Boston: Wisdom Publications, 1987).

Digha Nikaya, pp. 91–93: from Bhikkhu Bodhi (trans.), *The Discourse on the Fruits of Recluseship* (Kandy, Sri Lanka: Buddhist Publication Society, 1989).

Digha Nikaya, p. 107: from Geoffrey Parrinder (ed.),

SOURCES

The Wisdom of the Early Buddhists (New York:
   New Directions Publishing Corp., 1977).

The Flower Ornament Sutra, pp. 187–188: from Sangharakshita, *The Eternal Legacy* (London:
   Therpa Publications, 1985).

Fukanzazengi, pp. 156–160: from Nyogen Senzaki and
   Ruth Strout McCandless, *Buddhism and Zen*
   (Berkeley, Calif.: North Point Press, 1987).

Genjo Koan, pp. 161–169: from Kazuaki Tanahashi
   (ed.), *Moon in a Dewdrop* (Berkeley, Calif.:
   North Point Press, 1986).

Itivuttaka, pp. 112–113: from Sangharakshita, *The
   Eternal Legacy* (London: Therpa Publications,
   1985).

Khuddaka Patha, p. 114: from William de Bary (ed.),
   The Buddhist Tradition (New York: Vintage
   Books, 1972).

Lalitavistara, pp. 130–131: from William de Bary
   (ed.), *The Buddhist Tradition* (New York: Vintage
   Books, 1972).

Lankavatara Sutra, p. 136: from D. T. Suzuki (trans.),
   The Lankavatara Sutra (London: Routledge &
   Kegan Paul, 1932).

Lankavatara Sutra, p. 197: from William de Bary (ed.),
   The Buddhist Tradition (New York: Vintage
   Books, 1972).

SOURCES

Lotus Sutra, pp. 203–204: from Bunno Kato, et. al., (trans.), *The Threefold Lotus Sutra* (Boston: Tuttle, 1986).

Mahaparinibbana Sutta, pp. 116–117: from Maurice Walshe (trans.), *Thus Have I Heard* (Boston: Wisdom Publications, 1987).

Mahaparinibbana Sutta, p. 125: from T. W. Rhys-Davids (ed.), *Sacred Books of the Buddhists*, vol. 3 (London: Pali Text Society, 1977).

Mahavagga, pp. 58–60: from T. W. Rhys-Davids and Herman Oldenberg (trans.), *Vinaya Texts*, part 1, in *Sacred Books of the East* (Delhi: Motilal Bararsidass, 1968).

Majjhima Nikaya, pp. 26–27: from William de Bary (ed.), *The Buddhist Tradition* (New York: Vintage Books, 1972).

Majjhima Nikaya, pp. 32–34: from Nyanamoli Thera (ed.), *The Life of the Buddha* (Kandy, Sri Lanka: Buddhist Publication Society, 1978).

Majjhima Nikaya, p. 35: from E. A. Burtt (ed.), *The Teachings of the Compassionate Buddha* (New York: Mentor Books, 1955).

Majjhima Nikaya, pp. 44–45: from Nyanatiloka (trans.), *The Word of the Buddha* (Kandy, Sri Lanka: Buddhist Publication Society, 1971).

Majjhima Nikaya, pp. 100–101: from Christmas Humphreys (trans.), *Wisdom of Buddhism* (New York: Random House, 1961).

Mangala Sutta, pp. 12–15: from Gunaratana Mahathera (trans.), *Bhavana Vandana: Book of Devotion*. High View, W. Va.: Bhavana Society).

Milindapanha pp. 63–64: from Edward Conze (ed.), *Buddhist Scriptures* (New York: Penguin Books, 1959).

The Perfection of Wisdom in 25,000 Lines, pp. 191–192: from Edward Conze (ed.), *Buddhist Texts through the Ages* (Boston: Shambhala Publications, 1990).

Reflections on Sharing Blessings, pp. 127–128: from *Chanting Book* (Hertfordshire, England: Amaravati Publications, n.d.).

Rinzai roku, p. 186: from Irmgard Schloegl (trans.), *The Zen Teachings of Rinzai* (Boston: Shambhala Publications, 1976).

Samyutta Nikaya, pp. 16, 97–99, 122–123: from John Ireland (trans.), *An Anthology from the Samyutta Nikaya* (Kandy, Sri Lanka: Buddhist Publication Society, 1981).

Samyutta Nikaya, pp. 23–24: from Edward Conze (ed.), *Buddhist Texts through the Ages* (Boston: Shambhala Publications, 1990).

Samyutta Nikaya, pp. 32–34: from Nyanamoli Thera

(ed.) *The Life of the Buddha* (Kandy, Sri Lanka: Buddhist Publication Society, 1978).

Samyutta Nikaya, pp. 38–43, 53: from Nyanatiloka (trans.), *The Word of the Buddha* (Kandy, Ceylon: Buddhist Publication Society, 1971).

Samyutta Nikaya, pp. 54–56: from David Maurice (trans.), *The Lion's Roar* (New York: Citadel Press, 1967).

Satipatthana-sutta, pp. 70–77: from Thich Nhat Hanh, *Transformation and Healing* (Berkeley, Calif.: Parallax Press, 1990).

Song of Mahamudra, pp. 170–178: from Garma C. C. Chang (trans.), *Teachings of Tibetan Yoga* (New Hyde Park, New York: University Books, 1963).

Song of Zazen, pp. 205–207: from Robert Aitken, *Taking the Path of Zen* (Berkeley, Calif.: North Point Press, 1982).

Sutra of Hui-neng, pp. 193–196: from Philip Yampolsky (trans.), *The Platform Sutra of the Sixth Patriarch* (New York: Columbia University Press, 1967) and A. F. Price and Wong Mou-lam (trans.), *The Diamond Sutra and The Sutra of Hui-neng* (Boston: Shambhala Publications, 1990).

The Sutra on Full Awareness of Breathing, pp. 80–84: from Thich Nhat Hanh, *Breathe! You Are Alive:*

SOURCES

The Sutra on Full Awareness Breathing (Berkeley, Calif.: Parallax Press, 1988).

Sutta-nipata, p. 90: from Dines Andersen and Helmer Smith, *Sutta-nipata* (London: Pali Text Society, 1913).

Sutta-nipata, pp. 3, 66–68: from H. Saddhatissa (trans.), *The Sutta-nipata* (London: Curzon Press, 1988).

Sutta-nipata, pp. 22, 25, 29–31, 120–121: from E. Max Müller (ed.), *Sacred Books of the East,* vol. 10 (London: Oxford University Press, 1924).

Therigatha, pp. 94–95: from Susan Murcott (trans.), *The First Buddhist Women* (Berkeley, Calif.: Parallax Press, 1991).

The Tibetan Book of the Great Liberation, pp. 179–182: from W. Y. Evans-Wentz (trans.), *The Tibetan Book of Great Liberation* (London: Oxford University Press, 1954).

The Tibetan Book of the Dead, pp. 183–185: from W. Y. Evans-Wentz (trans.), *The Tibetan Book of the Dead* (London: Oxford University Press, 1960).

Udana, p. 79: from F. L. Woodward (trans.), *Minor Anthologies of the Pali Canon* (London: Oxford University Press: 1948).

Verses on the Faith Mind, pp. 144–155: from Richard

B. Clarke, *Verses on the Faith Mind* (Fredonia, New York: White Pine Press, 1984).

Vimalakirti Sutra, pp. 137–142: from Robert A. F. Thurman (trans.), *The Holy Teaching of Vimalakirti* (University Park, Penn.: Pennsylvania State University Press, 1976).

Vinaya Pitaka, p. 108: from F. S. Woodward (trans.), *Some Sayings of the Buddha* (London: The Buddhist Society, n.d.).

Vinaya Pitaka, p. 126: from Geoffrey Parrinder, *The Sayings of the Buddha* (London: Gerald Duckworth and Co., 1991).

Yogacara Bhumi Sutra, pp. 21–22: from Edward Conze (ed.), *Buddhist Texts through the Ages* (Boston: Shambhala Publications, 1990).

The Zen Teaching of Huang Po, pp. 200–202: from John Blofeld (trans.), *The Zen Teaching of Huang Po* (New York: Grove Press, 1958).

ACKNOWLEDGMENTS

The editors gratefully acknowledge permission to quote from the following works:

Breathe! You Are Alive: Sutra on the Full Awareness of Breathing by Thich Nhat Hanh. Adapted and re-printed with permission of Parallex Press, Berkeley, Calif.

Buddhism and Zen, by Nyogen Senzaki and Ruth Strout McCandless. Copyright © 1953, 1987 by Ruth Strout McCandless. Reprinted by permission of North Point Press, a division of Farrar, Straus & Giroux, Inc.

The Buddhist Tradition, edited by Wm. Theodore de Bary. Copyright © 1969 by William Theodore de Bary. Reprinted by permission of Random House, Inc.

The Dhammapada: The Sayings of the Buddha, by Thomas Byrom. Copyright © 1976 by Thomas Byrom. Reprinted by permission of Alfred A. Knopf, Inc.

ACKNOWLEDGMENTS

The First Buddhist Women: Translation and Commentary on the Therigatha, by Susan Murcott. Adapted and reprinted with permission of Parallax Press, Berkeley, Calif.

The Holy Teaching of Vimalakirti, translated by Robert A. F. Thurman (University Park, Penn.: Penn State Press, 1976), pp. 58–59, 61–62. Copyright 1976 by The Pennsylvania State University. Reproduced by permission of the publisher.

The Lion's Roar, copyright © 1967 by David Maurice. Published by arrangement with Carol Publishing Group, a Citadel Press Book.

Moon in a Dewdrop: Writings of Zen Master Dogen, edited by Kazuaki Tanahashi. Copyright © 1985 by the San Francisco Zen Center. Reprinted by permission of North Point Press, a division of Farrar, Straus & Giroux, Inc.

"Reflections on Sharing of Blessings," © Amaravati Publications.

Taking the Path of Zen, by Robert Aitken. Copyright © 1982 by Diamond Sangha. Reprinted by permission of North Point Press, a division of Farrar, Straus & Giroux, Inc.

The Tibetan Book of Great Liberation, translated by W. Y. Evans-Wentz (Oxford, England: Oxford University Press, 1954). Reprinted by permission of Oxford University Press.

Transformation and Healing: Sutra on the Four Foundations of Mindfulness by Thich Nhat Hanh. Adapted and reprinted with permission of Parallax Press, Berkeley, Calif.

ABOUT THE EDITORS

Jack Kornfield was trained as a monk in tem-
ples of Thailand, Burma, and India. He is a
practitioner and teacher of Insight Meditation,
the Buddha's path of mindfulness. He teaches
at Spirit Rock Center in Woodacre, California.

Gil Fronsdal is a Zen priest and has trained
as a monk in Burma. He is a practitioner and
teacher of Insight Meditation. He also teaches
at Spirit Rock Center in Woodacre, California.

For more information about Insight Meditation, contact:

> Spirit Rock Center
> 5000 Sir Francis Drake Blvd.
> Box 909C
> Woodacre, CA 94973

LIBRARY OF CONGRESS
CATALOGING-IN-PUBLICATION DATA

Teachings of the Buddha/edited by
Jack Kornfield with Gil Fronsdal.
— 1st ed.   p.   cm.—(Shambhala pocket classics)
ISBN 0-87773-860-2 (alk. paper)
1. Gautama Buddha—Teachings.
I. Kornfield, Jack, 1945–   .
II. Fronsdal, Gil.   III. Series.
BQ915.T43   1993   92-56457
294.3'63—dc20   CIP

SHAMBHALA POCKET CLASSICS

THE ART OF PEACE:
Teachings of the Founder of Aikido
by Morihei Ueshiba
Compiled and translated by John Stevens

THE ART OF WAR by Sun Tzu
Translated by Thomas Cleary

THE ART OF WORLDLY WISDOM
by Balthasar Gracián

AWAKENING LOVING-KINDNESS
by Pema Chödrön

BACKWOODS AND ALONG THE SEASHORE
by Henry David Thoreau

THE BOOK OF LEADERSHIP AND STRATEGY:
Lessons of the Chinese Masters
Translated by Thomas Cleary

DHAMMAPADA:
The Sayings of the Buddha
Rendered by Thomas Byrom

THE ESSENCE OF T'AI CHI by Waysun Liao

FLATLAND by Edwin A. Abbott

(Continued on next page)

HEALING MEDITATIONS by Tulku Thondup

HONEST BUSINESS
by Michael Phillips and Salli Rasberry

I CHING:
The Book of Change
Translated by Thomas Cleary

THE MAN WHO PLANTED TREES by Jean Giono

MEDITATIONS by J. Krishnamurti

NATURE and Other Writings
by Ralph Waldo Emerson

THE PATH OF INSIGHT MEDITATION
by Joseph Goldstein & Jack Kornfield

THE POCKET RUMI READER
Edited by Kabir Helminski

THE POCKET TAO READER
Translated by Eva Wong

THE POCKET ZEN READER
Edited by Thomas Cleary

POEMS by Emily Dickinson
Edited by Brenda Hillman

SAILING ALONE AROUND THE WORLD
by Captain Joshua Slocum

(Continued on next page)

ZEN LESSONS: The Art of Leadership
Translated by Thomas Cleary

For a complete list, send for our catalogue:
Shambhala Publications
P.O. Box 308
Boston, MA 02117-0308